M000307245

The 3 *Ships:*

Relation*Ships*, Leader*Ship* and Partner*Ships*

Randy L. Russell

Dear John,

Thank you - we've never met yet, but we are friends! I appreciate your friendship, leadership, and mentoring - you've had an impact on myself and my teams for over 25 years. Enjoy the 3 Ships my friend.

Randy

The 3 *Ships:*

Relation*Ships*, Leader*Ship* and Partner*Ships*

Randy L. Russell

Copyright © 2020 by RLR Leadership Consulting

RLR Leadership Consulting, LLC
12803 East 36th Avenue
Spokane, WA 99206
www.randyrussell.org

Printed in the United States of America

All rights reserved. No part of this publication may be reproduced, stored in a retrieval system, or transmitted in any form or by any means without the prior written permission of the publisher.

10 9 8 7 6 5 4 3 2 1
Library of Congress Cataloging-in-Publication Data
Names: Russell, Randy L., author.
Title: The 3 ships: relationships, leadership and partnerships
Description: Spokane: RLR Leadership Consulting, LLC.

Identifiers:
ISBN 978-1-09831-821-5 (print)
ISBN 978-1-09831-822-2 (eBook)
Subjects: Leadership
RLR Leadership Consulting
Randy L. Russell, Founder and President

Dedication

This book is dedicated to my family, friends, and mentors.

Thank you for always being there for me.

Acknowledgements

A special thank you to:

Shawna, Emily, Megan, Ryan and Rylee - "The Wind in My Sail."

Brian, Kyle, Doug, Gene and Rich for helping me discover and develop *The 3 Ships.*

Shelly Shaffer for her incredible insights and help.

My great friends, teachers, coaches, colleagues and mentors.

Contents

Figures

Foreword

Leadership matters, it matters a great deal. Leaders build capacity in people and organizations. They are the catalyst for transformative people and systems change. This transformational leadership does not occur by accident, it is a result of focused effort, imaginative thinking and a relentless personal commitment to self-improvement and continuous growth.

We live in uncertain times. Leaders today must peer through the fog of uncertainty and navigate uncharted waters that inspires confidence, hope and realism. These leaders minimize ambiguity. They prioritize, embrace, and model empathy and compassion while holding a steady hand on the essential skills of building, honoring and sustaining relationships, leading, and developing partnerships.

Dr. Randy Russell wrote the *3 Ships: Relationship, Leadership and Partnerships* for aspiring and seasoned leaders who want to build and create a legacy of lifting people and organizations to new heights. It is based on a combination of leadership skills the author learned in his vast experiences as a highly effective public-school administrator.

This book should be required reading for both the new and veteran administrators and supervisors. Randy provides valuable counsel, lessons-learned and experiences that are thorough, concise and practical in content and application. Dr. Russell provides time-tested leadership strategies that are pulled together in one valuable and easy to read format.

This book is about courage; courage to take on leadership positions in education; to lead with morals, values, and ethics as guiding principles. Randy speaks from experience and provides a practical, inclusive, and insightful guide for leaders in education. He provides a practical and realistic blueprint to follow for a successful career in educational administration.

This meaningful book provides a guide that will assist current and future leaders to develop a personal awareness of traits, values, and beliefs of successful leaders as they navigate a future of uncertainty with the essential skills of relationship, leadership and partnership building.

John Harris reminded us that, "If there is any common trait of failed leadership, it is the incapacity for growth – a reliance on old habits and thinking even when events demand the opposite." The *3 Ships: Relationships, Leadership and Partnerships* offers leaders new insights and the confidence necessary for leaders to navigate the sea of uncertainly into the calm of optimism and courage.

It is a must read for anyone who aspires to be an effective leader.

Dr. Gene Sharratt

Author's Note

While no one can claim to be the master of their own fate, everyone is the captain of their own ship. The ability, power, and skills to chart a course through life resides within each individual. Life isn't a solo voyage. Each one of us is *responsible* for both ourselves and our crew - our family, friends, staff, team, school, company, or organization. *The 3 Ships* focuses on Relation*Ships*, Leader*Ship*, and Partner*Ships* and will help grow and develop skills related to each, which will result in being happier both as a person and as a leader - at home, at work, and in life.

Regardless of which direction it's headed, a ship encounters different weather patterns during its voyage: smooth sailing, the doldrums, and storms. Life is unpredictable and ever-changing. As the captain of the ship, several instruments are necessary to successfully navigate safely from port to port.

People often experience a shipwreck (or two) in their lives. I've been living my own shipwreck – both personally and professionally – for the past four years. I have experienced enormous loss, failure, and suffering. My journey, like so many others' journeys, has been challenging. I have leaned heavily on my crew to help bring myself and others through these tumultuous experiences. *The 3 Ships* shares how relationships, leadership, and partnerships provide hope and direction to bring anyone's ship into the harbor, regardless of the crises and challenges they and their crew have faced along their journey.

In this book, I use stories, examples, and practical experiences to develop the skills and abilities necessary to successfully navigate the three ships - relationships, leadership, and partnerships. This book provides guidance for growth, development, and happiness as it relates to these three important concepts. At the end of each chapter, the reader will have an opportunity to reflect on the information, identify key concepts and strategies to refine their skills, and develop an action plan to succeed in their everyday life and work.

Additional resources and tools can be found at randyrussell.org.

Introduction:

Developing *The 3 Ships:*

RelationShips, LeaderShip and PartnerShips

I'm wired to help other people. My desire isn't to be rich, or famous, or a movie star. My desire is to be helpful, to be an encourager, and to be someone who makes a difference for others. I have seen first-hand the difference people can make in the lives of others. My hope and desire is to have my relationships, leadership, and partnerships help as many people as possible and make a huge impact on other people's lives. I also want to help other leaders have the same impact on people and make a difference in their lives.

This book, *The 3 Ships: RelationShips, LeaderShip and PartnerShips,* will address several key questions, including:

- Do you want to build and develop meaningful relationships?

- Are you ready to improve your leadership capacity and skills?

- Do you want to increase and strengthen your partnerships?

This book will help answer these three questions and strengthen relationships, grow and develop leadership skills, and identify and promote partnerships. The order of the three ships is intentional. The book begins with relationships because of their importance in our everyday lives. After relationships, it moves into leadership, which cannot improve without building successful relationships with the team. The book concludes with partnerships because partnerships rely on strong relationships and leadership within the community to be effective.

Relationships connect us to one another and provide a foundation for leadership and partnerships. Throughout the book, I will share stories and insights, diving into strategies and techniques which will help each reader to develop an action plan. As one develops more meaningful relationships, improves leadership skills, and increases partnerships – both personally and professionally – changes will occur for the better.

Whether leading a family, staff, team, company, or organization, relationships are the connection which brings leadership and partnerships together. *The 3 Ships* will aid each one of us in charting a course, reaching our goals, and having abundant success in our adventures. Through our connections, we will fulfill our desire to help as many people as possible, while becoming the person and leader we were meant to be. There is compelling evidence that relationships contribute to a long, healthy, and happy life. The relationships formed with other people are vital to our mental and emotional well-being, and survival. Key relationships help people live longer, deal with stress better, and have healthier habits. In Chapters 2 and 3, I will present research and guidelines that will assist the reader in building stronger relationships. In Chapter 4, I will share stories that illustrate how some of my own relationships have grown and developed.

Leaders help when things are going well and help even more during crisis, devastation, and difficulty. To find leaders, simply look around and find those who are helping others. On life's journey, we are destined to be helpful so we can make a difference in other people's lives. There is no greater feeling than lifting up another person. Leadership is also an important function of management which helps to maximize efficiency and achieve organizational goals. Leaders possess great discipline, and they want to inspire others to follow the same path. One's future and success depends on strong leaders and leadership abilities. Many people want to lead, they just don't know how. We know leaders aren't born - they are developed. In Chapter 5, the characteristics of effective leadership will be discussed, the challenges of leadership will be included in Chapter 6, and leadership insights and experiences will be shared in Chapter 7.

Teamwork is essential to success and at the core of teamwork is partnerships. Partnerships are fundamental. They bring a variety of groups together, make each individual group stronger, support one another to be better together, and mutually benefit all parties involved. *The 3 Ships* will help increase these partnerships. Research and guidelines related to partnerships will be shared in Chapter 8, and stories and experiences in Chapter 9.

Chapter 10 explores lessons learned from others about the three ships. There are many lessons we can learn about both what to do and what not to do in our relationships, leadership, and partnerships. Ensuring the ship(s) don't sink is important for every person – especially leaders. In every journey, the captain wants to bring their crew home safely, and into a secure harbor every time. Strategies for a safe harbor will also be discussed in Chapter 10.

This book will conclude with the development of an action plan based on the three ships: relationships, leadership, and partnerships. This action plan focuses on improving skills and abilities as a captain (i.e. friend, colleague, leader, administrator, team member, partner). The action plan includes pieces to assist and help the crew to flourish under our leadership. Whether leading a family, a group of friends, a staff, a team, a company, or organization, *The 3 Ships* will assist each leader in reaching their goals with amazing success.

Chapter 1: The Power of *The 3 Ships*

A couple years ago, I had lunch with two friends - Brian Talbott and Kyle Rydell - at Red Robin in Spokane, Washington. I seek their counsel when I have questions, knowing their intelligence will guide me in the right direction. These two gentlemen possess academic and emotional intelligence. They are inspirational and collaborative. They both bring insight to their collaborative leadership style which quickly enhances trust from all parties, including myself. The connection I have made with these servant leaders has taken our relationship - both personally and professionally - to a greater level.

That day at lunch, we talked about many things, including the next school year. Having been elected as the Washington Association of School Administrators State President for 2018-19, I needed their help. This position meant moving beyond district leadership and into state level leadership, and I needed a plan. The three of us talked about developing a platform for my year of leadership in the Washington Association of School Administrators as a way to unite Washington's 295 school district leaders around a common vision.

Authentic moments spent with these two men always leads me to learn from their wide range of skills. As we brainstormed, we agreed *relationships* were the foundation for everything and should be the centerpiece of the theme. We also concurred our *leadership* as school district leaders was critical to the well-being of our customers - our students, families, staff members, and communities. Finally, we also decided our *partnerships* were critical for school districts to be successful.

From this lunch meeting, we identified additional topics we felt could be a part of the theme for my term. With each new idea, we circled back to relationships, leadership, and partnerships. As we dove into the discussion, we discovered all three items had one thing in common - the word "ship." By the end of our meeting, we had landed on *The 3 Ships* as the theme for my presidency. *The 3 Ships* were the common link to pull everything together.

When used in tandem, the three ships create a powerful force. The theme of relationships, leadership, and partnerships helped unite state leaders with something they could get their heads around. It was straightforward, catchy, and easy to understand. Although relationships, leadership, and partnerships have influenced me my entire life, the development of *The 3 Ships* brought all three together. The three ships helped frame my leadership as the WASA President.

After serving my term, I realized the greater significance of the three ships as the momentum began to influence leaders across our state. The three ships were having impact in other agencies, beyond K-12 education. Brian, Kyle, and I also realized - as the three ships gained momentum in our state - we could use the theme to help level the playing field for everyone: every person, family, school, school district, company, organization, community, government, or nation. I realized that I could share the concept with additional leaders and provide a platform that others could learn from and take into their jobs and lives. This book shares what I've learned.

Chapter 2: Relation*Ships*

Relationships are like cars. We take them for granted until something goes wrong. Then we wonder what happened. The car may look fine on the outside, but the inside is in terrible condition. Even though there were signs, many signs, along the way that the car may need a tune-up, service, or even a major repair, we often fail to respond to a vehicle until it won't run correctly or needs major repairs. It is the same way with relationships - we can fine-tune them and tweak them, make minor repairs, but if we need to do major work to them, it is costly and often it is too late.

Ultimately, there are healthy and unhealthy, good and bad, successful and unsuccessful relationships. Over the course of the next three chapters, we will consider the following questions:

- Why do we need relationships?
- Why are some relationships *good*?
- Who do you have your greatest relationships with?
- Why are some relationships *bad?*
- What is the difference?
- Who is someone with whom you need to rebuild or repair your relationship?

Relationships are the fundamental glue for our society. We need relationships and rely on our relationships to connect with one another. Relationships are imperative for different reasons such as increasing our emotional well-being, creating stability, and learning how to be a good friend. In addition, having someone to count on in times of need or when we face challenges, taking away loneliness, and making us feel included are important. Each of our relationships elicit different responses in ourselves that help us to grow and learn about ourselves. Relationships often are the bond that holds us together during stressful situations. Without relationships, we would have a deadened spirit and a lack of connection to ourselves.

In this chapter, a variety of relationships will be discussed, the differences between good and bad relationships will be examined, and ways to develop, build, and cultivate relationships with anyone will be shared. The person who makes the biggest difference in any relationship is you. One can determine how to build, develop and, sometimes, repair relationships, and this chapter will help.

Relationships are the Foundation of Success

Solid relationships are a foundation for successful families, teams, companies, organizations, and in life. Most people have a desire for meaningful and important relationships (Taibbi, 2018). Children want to have a meaningful relationship with their parents. Parents want to have a meaningful relationship with their children. Spouses want to have a meaningful relationship with one another. Friends want to have meaningful relationships. Employers and employees want to have meaningful and important relationships. Companies want to have meaningful relationships with their customers. School administrators want to have strong relationships with their faculty and staff, while teachers want to build strong relationships with their students.

Relationships are built through connections with people in our lives, and a true relationship is with someone who accepts our past, supports our present, encourages our future, and loves us unconditionally. This advice defines many of the key characteristics of relationships. When someone accepts our mistakes, our dreams, and wants to share, it is the sign of true caring. Whether with our family, friends, students, customers, or employees, in order to build strong relationships, we must build strong connections. Throughout this section, I will discuss some of the characteristics of relationships that help to establish those connections.

Caring for One Another

One of the most important elements in life is showing others we truly care for them. There are many ways to show we truly care for one other. We show we care by being kind, present, supportive, available, and concerned. Different types of relationships require different kinds of support and caring.

For example, a top priority for parents is caring for our children. We love our children regardless of what they do or how they act. When our children come into this world, we help them and we take care of them. This care often includes making sacrifices so that our children can have what they need: clothes, shelter, food, and love. We let our children know that we love them and need them. As they grow older, we help them learn how to take care of themselves, and our caring includes letting them make mistakes and supporting them as they try out their independence. Even as they leave home and have children of their own, we know that no matter what, our children will always need us, and we will always be there for them.

For companies and organizations, taking care of employees and customers should be the highest priority. The relationship we have with our employees and customers is not the same as with our children, but when we take care of our employees, they feel our concern for their well-being. In turn, they will take care of the company or organization and its customers. Employees want to be led by caring, thoughtful leaders who value each person. Caring for our customers and employees is one of the greatest ways we can build relationships.

Our students, and their families, are our "customers" in education; as educators, caring for our students and their families is one way we can demonstrate how much we value our relationship with them. If there are no students, then there are no schools or school districts. We want to make real, lasting connections with the people we love and serve. We want our employees and customers (i.e. faculty, staff, and students) to know how much we care about them, and we can show we care about them by making strong connections. We make a difference every day by showing them we genuinely care for them and we are here to help and support them.

Our families, friends, staff members, teams, and organizations endure difficulties, loss, and extremely challenging situations. There will be crises and other challenges. Relationships provide support for the people we care about and spend the most time with. They will need us to help them, and we will be ready to answer their call. Regardless of the situation, human compassion makes the difference for anyone who needs extra support. Being compassionate shows sympathy and concern for someone else's misfortunes. Being empathetic is the capacity to understand or feel what another person is experiencing, putting ourselves in someone else's shoes, and taking the time to listen. When we show empathy to the people who mean the most to us and to those on our team, then we develop stronger relationships and stronger connections.

Earlier in the author's note, I alluded to a personal shipwreck I had experienced during the past four years. One of the events I referred to was when Shawna - my wife - and I lost three of our four parents in less than a six-month period of time. Shawna and I, along with our children, were in crisis. We were shipwrecked. During the time we were grieving our loss, we had incredible, supportive people who helped us – our crew. Their compassion and empathy helped us to make it through and "repair" our ship so we could get back on course. Figure 2.1 provides some questions to consider when you experience your own shipwrecks (see Figure 2.1).

Figure 2.1

Challenging and Difficult Situations: Personal Shipwrecks

Think about a challenge, difficulty, or maybe even a crisis that showed up in your life. Consider the following questions to reflect on the experience.
• Who showed compassion and empathy? • Which friends offered help? Which ones didn't? • Which friends wanted to help, but did not know how? • How did this experience help with your own ability to be more compassionate and empathetic with other people when they were facing difficulty?

Note: This figure provides a practice exercise to consider challenges and difficult situations that are often encountered in relationships. Consider these questions to examine your own challenges.

The caring relationships that I have created in my life helped my family and I to survive this difficult time. The support of strong relationships helped me to become a better friend, husband, and father because they showed me an example of how I hoped to support people. Regardless of the situation, person, or event one is dealing with in their life, showing others that we care about them makes a difference. A caring approach begins with being a caring and kind person.

Be Kind

Most people know the *Golden Rule*: treat others as you'd like to be treated. Because we would like people to be kind to us, we often have an expectation for people to treat us the same in return. Being considerate to one another sets a positive, caring tone which then leads to a positive, caring climate. When people believe they have value, feel important, and are a part of a positive, caring climate, they will reciprocate. In schools and classrooms, teachers, administrators, and staff must treat their students with kindness in order to build a strong relationship. By modeling kindness, students can learn to be generous and compassionate toward others.

No matter what the situation is, our thoughts, gestures, and comments have a big impact on those who are on the receiving end. It is easy to say the first thing that comes to our mind when we are upset or mad at someone else. But, we often don't comment when we are happy with someone or when they have done a great job. Building healthy relationships means reflecting before reacting and being careful with our words. Being considerate in what we say and how we say it is a sign of respect to other people.

What does being kind look like? It could be a smile, a pat on the back, a hug, or a thank you card. It could be as simple as genuinely asking someone, "How are you doing?" and then taking the time to listen and connect with them. This means the world to people. This can build relationships. Kindness is not fake, but it can be practiced and honed. Asking a colleague or friend "How can I help you?" also shows caring, and we build trust by following through on the helping action.

Let's continue to show each other how much we care – by being both nice and kind - to anyone we meet or see. Ask yourself: who can I be nicer and kinder to? Kindness and care can kindle our relationships with others. It is never too late to be kind. It is important to be kinder than necessary.

Time Together

No matter what, building relationships takes time. We need to spend time together. It might be at a family gathering, during a date night, at a company picnic, or in a virtual environment. It doesn't matter what it is - what does matter is spending time together. People want time together and they want to be able to connect, to talk with one another, and to see each other. People yearn to connect with others, and spending time together creates an opportunity for those connections to grow.

If we cannot connect in person, then there are other ways to connect. I remember when I joined Facebook years ago. It was the first time I had connected with people online, and I was impressed by the way I was able to connect with people I hadn't seen in years. With some of those people, I was able to use Facebook as a way to connect in person again, and with others, we continue to see each other's pictures and events online, and that's enough. Since we have access to technological tools today, we are able to connect with people over long distances in ways that hasn't been possible before. Virtual meetings, online collaborative tools, and other technology make it possible to work with colleagues, connect with friends and family, or long-distance mentors. Nothing will ever replace the importance of when we can see, touch, talk, smell, and hear another human being, but being able to connect with people we care about reminds all of us we are truly alive and important to others.

We must intentionally plan for time together so we can strengthen our relationships. We need time so we can develop our connections. Not only does the time together need to be intentional and consistent, it needs to be focused. In increasingly busy schedules, it is a must to get regularly scheduled time together. This starts with our calendar – it must be a priority. We value what we put in our calendar, and we protect it. We must make sure we protect our relationships no matter what.

Conclusion

When we started this chapter, I highlighted a need to be in meaningful and important relationships. Ultimately, I acknowledged that there are good and bad relationships, and that if we had a choice, most people would likely choose to have a good relationship. To continue to grow and develop relationships, one must show compassion, caring, and understanding; establish strong connections; and be willing to work hard to maintain them. In the Figure 2.2, you can develop an action plan for your relationships using strategies discussed in the chapter (see Figure 2.2).

Figure 2.2

Action Plan: Relationships

| What are your three takeaways from this section? |
| 1. |
| 2. |
| 3. |
| What are two strategies you will use to improve your relationships? |
| 1. |
| 2. |
| What steps will you take now? (Action Step for Relationships) |

Note: This action plan will help you to take next steps related to relationships based on the information shared in this chapter.

Use this action plan to make your relationships stronger by focusing specifically on caring, kindness, and time.

Chapter 3: Trust + Communication = Relationships

Trust and communication are building blocks for any great relationship. Trust and communication contribute to strong relationships with family, friends, and colleagues. Communication and trust supports the solid relationships we have with other people. When people are in "sync" with one another, the relationship positively impacts all of those involved. Even when two parties disagree in private, and there will often be disagreements, we must be on the same page in public. This is critical. Without this level of trust, there is no relationship.

In Chapter 3, I will build on more information about developing strong relationships. Some key characteristics in relationships are trust and communication. Earning, developing, maintaining, and keeping trust is vital for every leader. Our relationships are influenced by the level of trust we have with those in our life. When we hear a realtor speak about property, it is location, location, location. With almost every successful relationship, it is about communication, communication, communication.

Trust

Trust is important because it is the basis around which all human relationships revolve. In The NeuroScience of Trust, Zak (2017) found that building a culture of trust makes a meaningful difference. Trust is confidence in the honesty and integrity of a person or thing. Without trust, there is no strong or healthy relationship. We need trust because it provides us with the knowledge and support that we can count on someone or something - no matter what happens in our life. Important questions included in the sections that follow include:

- What is trust?

- Why do we need trust?

- Why do you need to trust other people?

As leaders, we must be very clear in our minds how we define trust, why we need trust, and why we need to be able to trust others. Trust is a critical piece of every relationship. The higher level of trust, the stronger the relationship. We've all heard the saying, "Rome wasn't built in a day." Well, the same thing applies to trust. Trust is built one day, one interaction at a time, and yet it can be lost in a moment because of one poor decision.

No Surprises. Another important factor that can create trust is the "no surprises" approach – where neither party is ever surprised or surprises the other person. It is the single most important way to build trust. There are times when people love surprises. Birthdays, a vacation, a new puppy, and seeing someone we haven't seen in a long time are fun surprises. These are great surprises. But, other than birthdays, a vacation, a new puppy, or seeing a long lost friend or relative don't surprise anyone. Even if the situation feels minor, take the no surprises approach. This not only develops trust, but it keeps the communication lines open.

Building Relationships through High Levels of Trust

In every relationship, there is a circle of trust and there are different levels of trust. Trust involves perceptions from both parties; not only do we gauge how much we trust somebody, but at the same time, they determine their level of trust with us. One might ask questions like: How is your trustworthiness? Can you be trusted? or Do you trust others? Based on this gauge of trust, we make a judgement call on whether the other person is inside or outside of our circle of trust.

The Elements of Trust. The four most common, fundamental elements needed to develop trust are competence, reliability, integrity and communication. Competence refers to the ability to do something successfully or efficiently. We are competent at developing relationships when we have successful ones. Reliability is the quality of being trustworthy or performing consistently well. When others know they can count on someone to keep their word, they relax and they don't have to keep their guard up. This level of reliability contributes to healthy relationships. The quality of being honest and having strong moral principles is integrity. Often our strongest relationships consist of people with whom we share the same values. We must be honest with people we have relationships with and this demonstrates a level of integrity that often develops into strong relationships. Finally, communication means the imparting or exchange of information. In order to create trust, we must be able to communicate with the other person. Communication means speaking and acting upon one's word.

There have been several different levels of trust that will be discussed below. These levels reveal important components of trust that relationships rely on. Carol Goman, Forbes Leadership Strategist, shares her "Six Levels of Trust":

- Trust in Yourself and the Value of Your Contributions

- Trust Between Team Members - Couples, Family, Friends, and Organizations

- Trust in the Team's Leadership

- Trust in the Importance of the Project or Assignment

- Trust in the Members of a Group and Employees

- Trust in the Collective Group (Goman, 2011)

Goman's six levels of trust will be discussed in more detail in the following paragraphs.

Trust in Yourself and the Value of Your Contributions. Goman (2011) claims human beings are a "teaching/learning species." We take pride in the specific knowledge we've accumulated, we enjoy adding to our expertise, and we get a psychological lift from communicating our knowledge to others. But to be a vital contributor, we must believe that our opinions and insights matter, and that our knowledge and experience are valuable to someone else. Unless people trust the innate wisdom and creativity of their ideas, there is little impetus to offer them to others.

I believe listening to others can support the development of self-trust. When people know we are truly listening to their ideas, they are more likely to share in the future, and this could assist in their ability to achieve this first level of trust.

Trust between Team Members - Couples, Family, Friends, and Organizations. Per Goman (2011), well-placed trust grows out of experience and interaction – usually extended over time. In fact, there are studies of the "mere exposure effect" which find that just seeing someone repeatedly -- making them more familiar -- increases our acceptance and trust of that person.

Effective team leaders have learned that the time to get to know one another and to build valuable "social capital" at the beginning of a project leads to building trusting relationships that pay off in increased productivity later on. This is where ice-breaker activities come into play in classrooms and office settings. Getting to know classmates, teammates, and co-workers before starting a big project or a new class can make a difference. If students don't feel safe in their classroom, they won't trust their teacher or other students enough to take risks. And, to learn, we all must take risks and move out of our comfort zones.

Trust in the Team's Leadership. Regardless of the overall corporate culture, individual managers and team leaders can create mini-cultures of trust within their work group or staff. The best of these leaders do so by taking the time and effort to make people feel safe and valued. They emphasize team cohesiveness while encouraging candid and constructive conflict. They set clear expectations for outcomes and clarify individual roles, and these expectations align with goals team members also share. When the team shares a goal and they know the leader is working toward that goal, they trust the leader to get them there. Strong team leaders help all members recognize each person's strengths. They tell stories of group successes -- and the lessons learned in failures. They share the credit and the reward or recognition. And, most of all, they encourage everyone's input, using body language that projects openness, inclusiveness and respect.

Trust in the Importance of the Project or Assignment. People are not likely to care about collaborating on projects they feel are unworthy of their contribution - a derisive term for this kind of project is WOMBAT -- Waste of Money, Brains and Time, as per Goman (2011). Conversely, human beings are more willing to share information when there is a compelling, emotional reason to do so or when working on a project they believe has real meaning and importance. Part of the leader's role is to clearly illustrate the organization's crucial business need for the fruits of a team's collaboration.

Unfortunately, in education, I have often experienced WOMBAT during professional development. The lack of follow through often makes in-service trainings for teachers and staff a waste of time because after the training, the concept is not revisited. This type of project feels more like checking a box than valuable development of skills. However, several times in my educational experience, I have attended a professional development or completed a project that had long-term impact on my work. I learned to be a better teacher or administrator as a result and it helped make the team I worked on even better than before. When this happens, it builds trust in the leadership and the project.

Trust in the Members of a Group and Employees. People learn what is important to leaders by the behaviors they see modeled by those leaders. Too often, there is a leadership "say-do" gap around the area of trust (Goman, 2011). Leaders can develop trust by creating an environment that demonstrates certain behaviors are valued. Rather than simply telling their team to act a certain way, but doing something completely opposite; a strong leader models actions that the team is expected to do.

Another way to build trust is to truly show interest in the opinions of others. When people hear leaders asking for participation or opinions, but then use exclusionary and dismissive body language that clearly shows they are actually uninterested in the opinions, this sends a negative message to the team. Employees need to hear leaders saying that knowledge sharing is essential, and see leaders trusting them by being candid and forthcoming.

Trust in the Collective Genius. Human beings thrive in collaborative relationships. Given the right context, they can do great things together. Goman (2011) claims there is a phenomenal sense of accomplishment in achieving as a group what could not have been achieved as individuals. But that won't happen unless everyone on the team understands and trusts that none of us is smarter than all of us.

To create a successful team, leaders must work to build the value of collaboration and be willing to spend time team building. We often see this demonstrated in sports, but collective achievements can also be accomplished in work and school environments.

Trusting Your Child to Drive the Car

When we are building trust with others, it is often built slowly. People give a little bit and see what happens, then they give a little more. For some, trust come easily. For others, trust is more difficult to garner. People have to earn it through their actions and deeds.

For example, as a young child, my parents allowed me to sit on their lap and control the steering wheel while we drove our car down the road to our house. It was fun to do, and there was no real accountability for me as my parents controlled the gas, the brake, or even the wheel if there was a problem. I trusted them to protect me, but as I got older, I realized there wasn't going to be anyone to control the gas, brake, or steering wheel if I got into trouble. I had to trust myself, and my parents had to trust me. I quickly realized driving was going to be my responsibility, and there would be no one else to take the controls if there was a problem. When I received my driver's license, my parents trusted me enough to be able to drive our car - a 1967 Chevy Impala - to school and around town. If my parents knew one-tenth of what I did while I drove our family car, they would never have allowed me get into the vehicle. But, as I gained experience and confidence, my driving skills improved and the trust that my parents had in my driving abilities grew.

I watched as others learned to drive and received their driver's licenses. One of my friends, David, who was three years older than me, had quite an experience learning to drive. On several occasions, I was in the back seat of David's Ford Bronco while he was practicing for his driver's license test. His mom was in the passenger seat teaching David how to drive. She wanted desperately to control the gas, brake, and steering wheel as David practiced. She often reacted as if she had the steering wheel, the gas, and the brake. A couple of times I thought she was going to break her knee cap when she rammed it into the dashboard in an attempt to pound her foot on the brake pedal. When we finished each practice drive, she had to get out of the car before she hyperventilated. David's mom struggled with trusting David's driving abilities, but we never crashed during the driving lesson. As David's driving abilities improved with more practice, he earned his mother's trust.

Learning to drive a car requires trust from many parties. Parents must trust their children will be safe and responsible with the expensive, heavy, dangerous machine they hold the keys to. Children must prove they are trustworthy by following driving rules and etiquette, as well as by demonstrating their ability to adhere to parental expectations about the vehicle. The community also trusts that the child is prepared to be on the road after they've passed their driving test and attended driving classes. Yet, society knows teen drivers are riskier on the road than seasoned drivers, and so, society also trusts that seatbelts, airbags, and other safety features on passenger vehicles will protect everybody in case of an accident. Obviously, trust must be considered from many viewpoints, and driving a car provides a great example of how trust impacts so many relationships.

Trust is Built during Crisis and Difficulties

Almost every leader inevitably faces a crisis during their voyage. Leadership often involves difficulties. Responses during a crisis or difficulty reveal essential characteristics about the leader. A steady, level-headed response to stress can build trust while a response that shows an inability to cope with stress can destroy trust. During adversity, our perspective determines our decisions. Looking at the bright side of a situation rather than allowing the negativity to dictate our emotions will make a difference in our relationships.

It is much easier for us to lead and serve when things are going well and when we're getting it right, but even harder to lead in tough times. The following historical example provides details about leading during tough times and building trust as a result. Sir Winston Churchill, the British Prime Minister (1940–45, 1951–55), rallied the British people during World War II and led his country from the brink of defeat to victory. His leadership skills were elevated during this difficult time, and he became the most trusted leader in England and one of the most trusted leaders in the world.

I've had several experiences of leading during crisis and difficulties. One example of building trust during a difficult situation occurred when I was serving as the Coeur d'Alene (ID) High School Principal. One of our students, known and loved by our entire student body, was battling terminal cancer. As the leader, I thought I was supposed to be tough, strong, and unaffected in this situation. I was anything but these things; I was a wreck emotionally and mentally. I did everything I could to keep myself together, let alone lead the school through this difficulty. The situation affected our entire school community, not only the students and people at the school. After talking with a dear friend, I decided it was best to stay true to myself. Our community saw how much I was truly hurting, and being vulnerable helped me to build trust with our students, staff, and community, and they saw firsthand how much I truly cared about this young man.

Our choices during times of crisis help to build or destroy trust. Both Winston Churchill and I learned to lead during times of crisis and our reactions to the difficult situations we both faced helped our communities to develop stronger trust in our leadership. The relationships we developed with our stakeholders as a result of the crisis worked to define our futures together.

Communication

Effective communication is the exchange of thoughts, information, ideas, and messages between people or groups. Communication is reciprocal, so it's depends on the transmission being understood by the receiver. "The Importance of Communication Skills" (Bundrant, 2019) outlines research studies on proven benefits of effective communication. Regardless of whether a conversation is at the kitchen table, in a staff meeting, at a sales meeting, or in the board room, two-way communication is critical for all parties to be successful. Leaders learn to listen and they listen to learn. In this next section, I will share the skills I believe are necessary for effective communication in any setting.

Necessary Skills

I believe there are five skills necessary for clear and effective communication – listening, speaking clearly, making a connection, empathy, and feedback. These five skills will help with everything from daily interactions to even the most difficult conversations. Listening means giving our attention to understand when someone is speaking. But, don't confuse listening with hearing; hearing is a physical ability, while listening is a skill. When speaking clearly, using the right words and the right tone is essential. The communication should also be in the right diction and pronunciation, in a manner that the receiving party understands. Making a connection is the process of developing a connection with the one being communicated to. This can include both a verbal and non-verbal connection. Empathy is the art of putting ourselves in another person's shoes to understand the emotion and perspective of the other person. Empathy helps us communicate in a way that will make sense to others. Feedback will benefit both the giver and the receiver. It helps in completing the communication process and influences a positive and productive outcome.

Clear, Concise and Consistent Communication. Have you ever played the game telephone? If you have, then you know the game begins with a large group of people getting into a circle. One person begins by whispering a message to the person next to them. The second person whispers exactly what they heard to the third person, and so on, until the entire group has heard and shared the message. Ultimately, by the time the final person hears the message, it has become jumbled from the original message, and more often than not, the final message does not even resemble the original message. If you haven't engaged in a game of telephone before, give it a try. The difference between the original message and the message at the end of the game is hilarious. This example demonstrates the importance of clear communication, and how even when people intend to communicate clearly to others, the message often changes based on how it's interpreted.

Communication can occur verbally, nonverbally, in writing, and through behavior as well as by listening and using feedback. Whether someone is networking, having a casual conversation, or closing the biggest deal of their corporate career, the art of communicating clearly and effectively should not be overlooked. One can go as far as to say, it is the fundamental difference between good and great results. Therefore, effective and clear communication is a fundamental concept of an individual's personal and professional relationships. In order to communicate clearly, concisely, and consistently, we must be cognizant of how both our verbal and non-verbal communication comes across with others. Once a person is keenly aware of both, they can begin to focus on concise and consistent messaging.

Building Relationships through Excellent Communication

Communication helps build relationships for several reasons. First, the more individuals listen, the more they learn about others' perspectives. Listening thoughtfully, without judgement or interruption, is also a show of caring and respect. With stronger connections, come deeper feelings of trust. Having empathy while providing and receiving feedback shows we care about another person and that what they have to share is important to us. When we combine trust with excellent communication, then we have the foundation for building a solid relationship.

My Communication Models. No matter who or what kind of audience we are addressing, the art of communication can be daunting. I was fortunate to have excellent models in my life who took an interest early on in my writing and speaking, the two forms of communication that I use most often. Each of these mentors demonstrated effective communication by showing me how to write and speak more effectively, either alongside me or by pushing me from the sidelines. Without help from these men, I may have struggled with my communication skills and become stranded - or shipwrecked - in my relationships. Through these relationships, I was able to learn to become a better communicator and to build my relationships with others.

Two teachers influenced my communication. I begin with Mr. Pond, one of my favorite high school teachers (see Chapter 4), who was my inspiration to become a better writer and speaker. Not only did he help me become a more detailed writer, he helped me work through the fear of public speaking. I still get nervous when I speak in front of large crowds, and I still use his tips to work through the nervousness. From Mr. Pond, I continued my journey in becoming a stronger writer and speaker in college. Professor Wolf, a college professor from whom I took five classes, helped further develop my writing and speaking skills and challenged me to be much better than I thought I could be. Coming out of high school, I thought I was a decent speaker and writer; yet, Professor Wolf gave me a "C" on my first college paper. When I asked him about the grade, his comment was, "Welcome to College English, Mr. Russell." Professor Wolf helped me build on the great teachings of Mr. Pond. Not only did I highly respect them as teachers/instructors, but I really appreciated how they helped me become a better communicator.

As I continued to evolve as a public speaker and communicator, I was able to work with professionals in my field who mentored me to become better at this skill. Dr. Don Wattam, my doctoral thesis advisor and college professor, was instrumental in mentoring, helping, and supporting me as I earned my Ph.D. in Educational Leadership and while writing my doctoral thesis. His balance of high expectations with brutal honesty really helped me transform a written document into a published thesis which has driven some of my work as a school district superintendent. Along every step of my life and career there have been individuals who have lifted me up, and Dr. Don saw something inside me and lifted me to a level I didn't even know existed.

From there, I was able to learn from Dr. Michael Dunn, a long-time mentor, friend, and colleague. He has also been instrumental in the development of my writing, speaking and listening skills. With Dr. Dunn, I was able to move toward writing professionally, and he has helped me edit several articles and coauthor several others. Watching him and learning from him has been both educational and inspirational.

Through my journey, I have been able to improve my communication through strong mentors who have been willing to share their knowledge, skills, and expertise. Without Mr. Pond, Professor Wolf, Dr. Wattam, or Dr. Dunn, I may not have been confident enough in my writing skills to attempt this book. Their mentorship and guidance has provided me with the confidence to continue improving my writing and communication skills. Today, I spend time speaking in public and leading workshops regularly. I lead large groups of educators in my district and at the regional, state and national levels, and I am prepared to share my knowledge through written work, such as this book.

Conclusion

In this chapter, we explored the building blocks of relationships: trust and communication. In the action plan for this chapter, please think about how you can build trust and communication in your relationships. The steps that were outlined to create trust and stronger communication can provide you with ideas for action in your life. In the action plan included in Figure 3.1, please complete your steps to creating better trust and communication in your relationships (see Figure 3.1).

Figure 3.1

Action Plan: Trust and Communication

What are your three takeaways from this section?
1.
2.
3.
What are two strategies you will use to improve your trust and communication?
1.
2.
What steps will you take now? (Action Step for Trust and Communication)

Note: This action plan will help you to take next steps related to relationships based on the information shared in this chapter.

Relate your action plan to what you've learned so far about building strong relationships, and this knowledge can be applied in Chapter 4 as I share personal stories and experiences related my relationships.

Chapter 4: Relationship Insights and Experiences

In the following chapter, several kinds of relationships will be discussed in more detail. Relationships aren't always easy, but we can learn from our relationship challenges, insights, and experiences. My relationship experiences continue to shape who I am, how I lead, and how I continue to build and develop as many positive, mutually beneficial relationships and partnerships as possible. Through the sharing of personal examples and stories, I hope to illustrate how relationships shape our identities.

Section 1: KinShip

Each one of us has a kinship with our family members. Kin relationships are traditionally defined as ties based on blood or marriage. Kinship includes lineal generational bonds (children, parents, grandparents), collateral bonds (siblings, cousins, nephews and nieces, aunts and uncles), and ties with in-laws (Reis & Sprecher, 2009). A family dynamic influences each one of us and provides a foundation for all other relationships in our lives. In this next section, I will share information about my family with the hope of creating personal reflections for readers based on kinship.

Relationships with Parents

Our parents are our first teachers, but their teaching jobs are never complete. Their jobs are 24 hours a day, 365 days a year, from the first day to the last. There is no official manual on how to be a parent although there has been plenty written about parenting. Children's relationships with their parents are often based on the premise that parents have their children's best interests at heart. My parents did their very best; your parents probably are doing, or did, their very best, too; and as a parent, we will try our very best, as well. However, sometimes parents – and children - make mistakes, which can damage relationships or make them stronger.

My Parents. As a young child, my siblings and I were with my parents all the time. The only time we weren't together as a family was when my dad was working. I remember, my parents always made time for us, and our family was their number one priority. The time we spent together helped to make our relationship stronger. We had a phenomenal relationship based on trust, respect, and mutual admiration.

Parental relationships are often protective. One experience I recall was when my dad literally kicked a mouthy neighborhood kid off the front steps of our house. It was like watching a movie or a video in slow motion; I can remember it like it happened yesterday. Even though I would never recommend dealing with a neighborhood bully in this way today, my dad didn't worry about the consequences – only about protecting my sister.

My older sister, Renee, was being harassed by some unruly neighborhood kids. At the time, she was in junior high, and some of the kids were being pretty mean to her. My dad told us, "Be on the lookout...If any of the neighborhood kids who are giving Renee a bad time show up, let me know." Clearly, if someone showed up in our yard, he was going to take care of it. Eventually, one of the neighbor kids came and rang our doorbell. My sister answered the door, and my dad was within earshot. The young man said something that wasn't appropriate to my sister. My dad rushed through the doorway, grabbed this young man by his plaid jean jacket collar, and drop-kicked him off the steps out into our front yard, all while yelling at the boy never to show his face near our house again. When my dad walked back into the house, my mom nervously asked what he had done. Not missing a beat, my dad said to all of us, in a soft, gravely tone, "You only get one family and you must protect it." After a long pause, he continued, "Because no one else will." This is the first lesson I remember learning about loyalty and looking out for your family. Another lesson I learned that day was that when my dad said he was going to do something, then he was going to do it. From this incident, we all knew we could count on Dad to protect us, and we knew we could count on him to always keep his word.

Like most children, my relationship with my parents had a few challenges as well. I remember trying to challenge their authority as parents. When those times occurred, not only did I learn valuable lessons, but it strengthened our relationship.

One clear memory is when I had just graduated from high school. Even though I was heading off to college in the fall, I was still living under my parent's roof and my parent's rules. My dad told me I could have an extra hour in the summer for curfew, telling me he needed me home by 1 a.m.

A good friend of mine had his brother's 1984 Jeep, and we decided to go out. We stayed up much later than we should have because we wanted to be with our friends, we thought we were cool, and apparently, we thought we could. We should have been in by 1 a.m., but instead I broke curfew, and my parents were upset. The next morning my dad didn't say much. His exact words were, "Out a little late last night, weren't you?" I apologized to him profusely, saying, "I can be trusted and I won't miss curfew again."

Even though I had every intention of keeping my promise, I disappointed them again. Ten hours later, I asked my parents if I could go out again. I could tell by the look on their stoic faces they were concerned, yet I assured them I was going to be able to make curfew that evening. My parents reluctantly gave me permission to go out again. Not only did I miss curfew, I didn't even come home. I ended up staying the night at my friend's house. When the phone rang later, I knew immediately it was my dad who had called. The thought of his face being as red as an apple and steam coming out of his ears, made me jump out of bed. Although he hadn't talked to me, I knew I needed to get home. So after sleeping for just a couple of hours, I drove home to see my dad waiting for me in the front yard. As I pulled to a stop, my dad was staring at me. What he did next is a lesson I have never forgotten. He handed me an axe and pointed at a pile of wood he and I had hauled in for the winter. My dad then stated, "The woodpile doesn't know the difference between whether you made it or didn't make it in for curfew last night. I know and most importantly, you know." He said if I told someone I was going to do something, then I needed to do it. No excuses. That day was one of the worst days of my life. I ended up chopping wood the entire day, with only water to drink and no food or breaks. As darkness settled in, my dad turned on some exterior lights. Finally, I was out of wood to chop. My dad walked outside. He told me that even though he was upset with me about the choice I'd made, he still loved me.

Although I had never missed curfew before, and I never missed curfew after that night, I had let my mom and dad down. It could have damaged our relationship because they were disappointed, but even in their disappointment, my parents still loved me. This experience showed me that parents love their kids no matter what. Even if they don't like some of the choices their children make, and even when we disappoint them, the relationship we have with our parents cannot be destroyed. But, both parties have to be willing to work on the relationship. My parents are no longer living, but the lessons they taught me are with me every day. I disappointed them and they didn't like every choice I made, but I know they loved me regardless of my choices. Some of the lessons I learned from my parents included honesty, hard work, and treating people with respect.

Parents of Others. During my career, I've experienced great relationships with many of the parents of students and athletes in the schools and school districts under my leadership. By far, the positive experiences outweigh the negative experiences. As a leader, we must remind ourselves of the positive interactions so they offset the negative experiences. In addition, we must remember that parents can teach educators and school leaders valuable lessons.

One lesson I learned through my years in education is that every parent is doing the very best they can for their child. I have witnessed many teachers and administrators adopt deficit mindsets when students arrive at school hungry, dirty, or unprepared, but I learned to remind myself that parents are sending us their very best: their children. And kids don't come to school to fail; they come to school to learn. So, we have to work hard so they know we are doing our very best to help them learn. The relationship between the school and its families is integral to students' success.

Family

Every family has their own three ships. The family relationships we have shape us, influence us and make us who we are. Whether the relationship is with a grandparent, aunt, uncle, parent, sibling, cousin, spouse or child, how we treat each other and how we act toward each other becomes a part of our family bond. Some families are small and nuclear, while others include large, extended relationships. In other families, children may have a stronger relationship with one parent or the other. One sibling might be closer to another sibling. Some families split up through divorce, some families grow through remarriage. Some families live hundreds of miles apart, others live right around the corner. All of these factors impact the relationships between the people in the family.

We don't get to choose our parents or our siblings. We don't get to pick our children. We don't choose our crazy "aunt" or "hard to get along with" cousin. Although we do have some control over who becomes our spouse, after we've created a family with somebody, the relationship we have with that person will always remain. Unlike family, we do get to choose the relationships we create with others.

Section 2: FriendShip

Friendship is another essential relationship and some people rely more heavily on their friendships when relationships with their family or parents is not strong. Friends often take on the role of family members and become a part of a relationship that resembles a family-type bond. Personally, as I was growing up, a couple of my best friends became a part of my family, even though we weren't related.

Friends come and go, but our true friends stick with us through thick and thin. Or they don't. It is important for us to surround ourselves with friends who will take us up, not down. This advice addresses the notion that friendships should be supportive. True friends are not jealous of each other; rather, they want their friends to succeed—even when a friend's success overshadows their own. People have a tendency to show their true colors when things go badly. They seem to be good friends when things are fine, but many of them are nowhere to be found when things get tough. We know we have a true friend when they are still with us after a true difficulty or challenge—even more so, we know our true friends through the actions they take during the crisis. For example, when my family experienced the crisis of losing loved ones, our true friends stood by us. Those friends that helped us through our tough time didn't expect anything in return; they just gave us their love and support.

Modeling friendly behavior can impact our relationships with friends. When we act like a good friend, we are more likely to attract good friends, but when we don't act like a good friend, the likelihood of somebody else acting friendly toward us is diminished.

My Friends

I've known my closest friends for twenty, thirty, or even forty years. We've been with each other through great times, death, divorce, celebrations, crisis, weddings, and births. Each of these - whether they are devastating or uplifting – has tested our friendship.

Many of my closest friendships are connected to sports. We either played on the same teams, we played against each other, or we coached together. Billy, Bryan, David, Kenley, Kenny, Rod, Terry, and Todd are those guys. A couple of us played on the same teams or played against each other going all the way back to Little League Baseball when we were ten years old. A few of us played together for a couple of years, and others, I played with all of the way through college. A couple of these guys I coached and then we served on the same coaching staff. Through many interactions across the years, we have grown close together, we mutually respect each other, and we have come to trust each other as friends, teammates, and colleagues.

We are as connected today as we were over forty years ago. The connections I've experienced with my friends include memories, competition, and wins and losses on the field and off. Through it all, these friends have been there for me no matter what, and I've been there for them. We are connected – literally – to this day. For example, on any given day, I'm either texting or talking to at least one of them, and some days, all of them. And, we are connected – emotionally – through our strong relationships. Our love for each other is as deep as any family relationship, and I consider them to be my brothers.

Relationships with friends don't always last. There will also be experiences where we will lose friends. We might lose a friend because of an argument, broken trust, other unfortunate situation, or we might also lose a friend because they pass away. Two of my best friends have died, and it has impacted me in ways I never knew possible. When I was only eleven, my best friend at the time, Dino, died tragically in a skiing accident. I lost another one of my best friends just a few years ago when he committed suicide. I spoke to Troy hours before he killed himself, and I had no idea he was in such pain. It still haunts me that he is gone. When we lose friends, we experience many emotions, and when we lose somebody tragically, those emotions are amplified.

I've been very fortunate to have such great friends in my life. My closest friendships mean everything to me. We have such great memories from our childhood, high school, college, and as adults. No matter how we stay connected, I have built relationships with my friends based on trust and loyalty. I know I can count on them, and they know they can count on me. That is a sure sign of a healthy friendship.

Section 3: MentorShip

Relationships are complicated and often go beyond kinship and friendships. Our relationships might include some sort of mentorship. As adults, we often take on the mentor role, but as children, adolescents, and adults, we are also often mentored by others. This is true with the mentoring relationships I have had in my lifetime. My mentors have allowed me to ask questions, provide insight, and then push me on my way. Great mentors don't take over at the helm of the ship; rather, they are guides who help to provide roadmaps and suggestions along the way.

Each leader has most likely been served by a mentor at some time in their life. A mentor can be a friend, colleague, relative or someone who might be assigned as a mentor. In "Why Mentors Matter: A Summary of 30 years of Research," Lauren Bidwell (2016) shares research about mentorship and its impact on future relationships and success.

In terms of relationships, mentorship is a complicated form. It's not always an equal give and take since so often one of the people is an "expert" while the other is a "novice." Research shows that strong mentors can help mentees improve their career outcomes, improve employee engagement, increase employee retention and support employee inclusion (Bidwell, 2016). It is often through mentors that people learn how to form better relationships with those around them, to manage a new job, and to create partnerships. As mentoring relationships grow, the mentee becomes independent and the mentor's duty often becomes obsolete as the mentee no longer needs mentoring. However, when this happens, the mentor can proudly watch that person become independent, and perhaps even go on to mentor others.

Consider for a moment the questions posed in Figure 4.1 (see Figure 4.1).

Figure 4.1

Mentors

Think about one of your mentors.
Were they good or bad mentors?
Were they great mentors?
What made them bad, good, or great mentors?
What are the characteristics of great mentors?

Note: This figure poses questions about mentors.

These questions ask you to personally connect with the concept of mentorship. Most of us have had an adult (i.e. a teacher, a coach, a friend, family member) who has taught us how to navigate certain situations in life. By considering the characteristics of one of these people, you will begin to know what it takes to be a great mentor.

Teachers, Counselors, Administrators and Coaches

One of the most important relationships people experience in their lives transpires at school. Our teachers can influence our personal and intellectual identities, and a great teacher can change lives. We are fortunate to have dedicated, committed, and caring educators who support students across the globe. I love educators; they teach despite poor funding, bad publicity, and long hours. They teach even though pressures and fear envelope U.S. classrooms. They teach because they love children, and they love learning.

If somebody asked, "Who was your favorite teacher?" Almost everybody has an immediate answer. They might even have more than one answer. Most people would not only be able to tell someone the name of this teacher, but could also share the grade and/or subject the teacher taught. As a follow up question, "Why were they your favorite teacher?" might reveal even more about this teacher and the relationship he or she established with you. The answer to the second question would most likely connect to how that teacher treated us, whether they believed in us, or how they made us feel. When I've asked this question, rarely has someone said the reason they were my favorite teacher is because "they taught me how to solve an equation" or "they taught me how to write a paragraph." The answer to this question invariably relates to the relationship between the teacher and the student.

Mr. Pond. Although I have had outstanding teachers as a student, one of my absolute favorites is Mr. Pond. Mr. Pond was my English teacher during my junior and senior year of high school, and he was also my tennis coach. I admired Mr. Pond, and I still do because he is all about relationships. He loved his students, wanted the very best for them, and brought out the very best in each, including me. I flourished because of Mr. Pond.

During class, Mr. Pond wasn't concerned about how students fared against other students; he was focused on developing our skills based on our potential. One of his favorite questions to ask was, "Are you doing the very best you can?" This was usually followed by, "How do you know?" He emphasized that we would always know if we were doing our very best. Mr. Pond believed in me – and all of this students - and this belief helped me understand that to be my best I would need to give my best. I have never forgotten this lesson, and it has impacted my effort, especially when faced with difficult tasks, ever since.

Hopefully, your experience was as great as mine was. I know teachers that were the most memorable to me treated me with respect, had high expectations for me, made me feel like I was important, and were there to help me in any way they could. Most likely, the teacher you thought of did the same. Wonderful, caring teachers can make a difference in the lives of students whose other relationships are damaged. A teacher cannot take the place of a parent, for sure, but a teacher can become a mentor and an ally for students that need this type of support.

Coaches. Another form of mentorship takes place on baseball diamonds, on football fields, on basketball courts, and at other athletic venues. Coaches are teachers, but they are at an advantage in some ways because they are teaching a content area that the player is interested and motivated in. But, coaches, like teachers, have the power to make a difference in both positive and negative ways.

Coach Embery. Coaches have been instrumental in helping me become who I am. As a former athlete and coach, when I refer to coaches, I include people who have coached me, as well as individuals I've been fortunate to coach with. Not only do I have a memory about each coach, but I have a story about each coach that is connected to a life lesson. They were excellent coaches and, more importantly, they were great mentors.

One of my college baseball coaches, Coach Embery, rode me like a wet mule for my entire sophomore year of college. I literally thought he hated me. One day after another practice where I was on the receiving end of Coach Embery's wrath, I asked him if I was doing something wrong or if he even liked me. He said, "Russell, as long as I'm yelling at you and staying on you to improve, then everything is fine. You only need to be worried if I'm not talking to you." Well, he *talked* to me all season long. It felt like his lips were attached to my left ear for the entire season, so I knew everything was fine although the stress of being chewed out regularly was difficult.

After the season was over, Coach and I met and he commended me for working hard and for sticking with it. He said, "Now, you're ready." I wasn't sure what that meant until he revealed that several scholarship offers to play baseball at the next level were headed my way. It was then that I realized the lessons I had been taught that year. Coach cared enough to get the very best out of me because he knew what I was capable of doing, even when I didn't completely understand myself. On the way out of his office, Coach said, "Russell, by the way, I do like you." We both smiled as I walked out the door.

Not only was I able to continue to play baseball at Whitworth University for my junior and senior year of college, I was able to stay on as a coach after graduating and eventually become the Head Baseball Coach at Whitworth. There have been many times I have told my players, my children, and even staff members the same words Coach Embery used on me: "You only need to be worried if I'm not talking to you." Each time I have said this, it has brought a smile to my face, and my mind has turned to the man we all called Coach.

Mr. Baird. Another important mentor in my life was my high school librarian and coach, Mr. Baird. Extremely strict and very disciplined, Mr. Baird had graduated from the same high school I attended and then joined the military. The training he received in the military - strict, disciplined, focused - was the same way he coached his student-athletes. He's the only coach I know who conditioned his athletes before a game.

During my junior year in high school, our varsity basketball team was having an outstanding season. The team was comprised of a great group of athletes who truly cared about each other and played very well together. Halfway through the season, Mr. Baird pulled my best friend, David Hillman, and I into his office to talk.

This was an exciting conversation with such a serious man. No team in the history of our high school had the opportunity to go as far as we could, and Mr. Baird wanted our team to make history. The reason he talked to the two of was he believed in us and our leadership abilities. He asked David and I: "Do you believe you could play for and win a state championship?" David and I unanimously agreed we could. Mr. Baird then asked us a very important question, "What could get in your way from winning it all? And, how will the two of you make sure that doesn't happen?" Again, David and I agreed the only thing that could get in our way was ourselves. We knew that we were going to need everyone. And, when we heard two of our players were rumored to be partying during the season, Mr. Baird told us if we wanted this bad enough, then we were going to have to tackle it head on because that is what true leaders do - they lead and tackle difficult challenges in their life.

We did exactly as Mr. Baird encouraged us to do. David and I talked to our two teammates, and they not only listened, but they agreed we had a once in a lifetime opportunity. They stopped partying. We had a great rest of the season, and we got into the state championship game - only to lose it by one point. This is one of my most vivid memories, where I felt like my leadership, and the mentorship of a wonderful coach, truly made a difference. In competition we either win or learn.

After my sophomore year of college (the year of heckling from Coach Embery), I returned to Montana for the summer to direct a baseball camp in the Flathead Valley of Montana. I met with Mr. Baird one of the days I was there. In our conversation, he asked me what I was going to do after I graduated from college, and I told him I was going to go to law school. Without missing a beat, he said, "Are you sure you want to be a lawyer? Randy, I think you should go into education." After that, Mr. Baird shared with me every reason why he went into education, including many positives and a few negatives, as well. He said the salary wasn't very good, but the experiences would be priceless. After a couple of hours talking, he and I created my future plan as an educator. He told me I was a connector, and I was good at helping people. He told me these were the reasons why I should go into education: I was great with kids; I needed to teach and coach; and I could make a difference in people's lives.

He was correct... as usual. Not only did he change the trajectory of my life, he reaffirmed his belief in me and taught me a valuable lesson about "tapping someone on the shoulder" when they see value and potential in another person. Looking back at this discussion with Mr. Baird, I think often about how it was a turning point in my life.

Colleagues. My colleagues have also made a difference in my life. The relationships I have with them often fall under friendship, but at times, they are also my mentors, as well.

Harry Amend and Dr. Gary Livingston. When I think of mentors in my life, I immediately think of two great men, Harry Amend and Dr. Gary Livingston. They are both amazing people and leaders who always focused their time and energy on building relationships, helping others, serving others, and developing their team members. These gentlemen have been able to build lifelong relationships with many people across their lifetimes because they truly care about people. They mentored and developed their leaders and teams while working full-time; yet, their mentorship continues to this day, even during retirement. Their focus on relationships is a great example for me, and I've applied their example to my own personal and professional relationships.

I've known Harry since he drove into the Flathead Valley in his family station wagon back in the early 1980's, while I was still in high school. Harry was a K-12 educator for over forty years and also worked as a professional baseball scout for many years. He signed two of my teammates to professional baseball contracts and helped dozens of young men, including myself, advance their baseball careers. Later in our lives, he also mentored many of us as we started jobs in education, school administration, business, the clergy, or in the military. Next to my dad, I look up to Harry more than anyone on the face of the planet. Harry is a connector - he's also one of the greatest human beings I've ever known. Anyone who knows Harry will say exactly the same thing. Harry is the type of Captain anyone would want to set sail with.

Dr. Gary Livingston might be one of the most respected people and leaders I have ever worked with in education. Gary and I have known each other for over twenty years. He was a fine teacher and administrator, but more importantly, he is a fine human being. He focused on relationships, then leadership. He also knew how to develop partnerships that mutually benefited all parties involved. He's still mentoring me as well as many other leaders in the field to this day. His tireless dedication to serving others and his willingness to help others get better is a testament to who he is. His mentorship of teachers and administrators over the years has improved the field of education, and so many of his mentees have gone on to great things

Dr. Gene Sharratt. Over the years I have learned several great lessons from my good friend and mentor, Dr. Gene Sharratt. Gene is also a hero of mine. He demonstrates strong family relationships; experience in various leadership positions, including as a platoon leader in Vietnam, and personal strength as a survivor of cancer. Gene's experience and wisdom can be measured by the countless others he has helped.

One of his most important sayings is, "You can't influence those you've offended." He is correct and since relationships and leadership are connected to influence, we should all try hard not to offend people. But, Gene also models ways to forgive ourselves and to ask for forgiveness if offense does occur. Relationships may incur conflict and difficulty at times, but Gene exhibits his ideology to create strong connections with people through his willingness to take responsibility for his mistakes and successes.

Gene's wisdom follows me around like insight I have gained from so many of my other mentors. He says, "If you want to go fast, go alone; if you want to go far, go together." He's right. There are many times when we want to go fast in order to complete a task or mark something off our "to-do" list. However, the real opportunity is in doing it as a team. It may take longer, but the reward will be richer. People will feel great knowing they contributed to something bigger than themselves. Gene is one of the most positive leaders I've ever been around. Gene makes me feel valued and important – like my contribution to the team is essential. His greatest satisfaction is in lifting others up and seeing the team succeed. He often shares with others the positive statement: "I'm a better person because of you." When I hear this statement, I think, "We are all better because of Gene."

State Leaders. At the beginning of this book, I mentioned my two great friends, colleagues, and mentors, Brian and Kyle. How lucky did I get? Meeting Brian and Kyle was like winning the lottery.

Kyle and I met at a new Superintendent training in Olympia, Washington. We arrived in the packed parking lot at the same time, with our short sleeved shirts, ties, and dress slacks on. We immediately knew we were going to the same training (or a summer wedding located nearby). When we met in that parking lot, we had an instant connection. Kyle's personality is like a magnet; he's positive, caring and motivated. He is all about relationships, leadership, and partnerships, and I continue to be impressed by the kind of person and leader that Kyle is. Watching Kyle and being able to ask questions, and receive advice from him has helped me become a better leader. Kyle and I first met as colleagues, but he has become a dear friend, colleague, and mentor.

Brian and I met under different circumstances. Brian had no choice, and little did he know what he was in for, when he was assigned to mentor me during my first year as a new superintendent. We not only connected and hit it off immediately, almost ten years later, he is still my mentor. Whether a tough personnel issue, a difficult budget decision, or the loss of a student, Brian has always been there for me as a mentor, and through our relationship, we've also become dear friends. Relationships mean everything to Brian, and he puts himself out there to take care of other people. When most others are walking away from challenges or crises, Brian heads toward the challenge. Most importantly, he has earned my unequivocal trust throughout the years.

I admire and respect both Brian and Kyle, and they are role models who helped me on the journey to discovering *The 3 Ships*. Without their mentorship, and that all-important conversation at Red Robin, *The 3 Ships* might not have been born. Their mentorship pushed me to become a better leader, and I hope to raise others through this book.

Section 4: Difficult Relationships

In our relationships with others, we don't always have positive relationships with everybody. We are not required to love everyone and have an excellent relationship with everyone we come across, and they are not required to like us, either. That's ok. Even if we don't particularly like someone or care about them, we might still be expected to maintain a professional relationship with that person. Sometimes in our relationships, we struggle with communication or with resolving conflicts. We must try even harder to treat these people with respect and kindness.

Even the kindest, most thoughtful people don't have great relationships with everybody. We might ask:

Why do we have enemies?

Why don't some people like us?

Why are there some people we don't like?

There are reasons. Sometimes there might even be good reasons. Some people are going to do things we don't like, such as breaking our trust, not following through, being too quiet or too loud. Not everybody we work with in our lives will become our best friends. Sometimes the relationship will simply be professional, but that doesn't change the fact that we must work with them and learn how to be productive members of the team despite our dislike for one another personally.

I love being an alumnus from Whitworth University. Attending school as a student, being able to serve there as an assistant coach, instructor, head baseball coach, and assistant athletic director brings back so many great memories. This hasn't always been the case. After my third very successful season as the head coach, we had a change in leadership when the university's popular athletic director retired. Not only had he hired me, but we had an excellent relationship. When the new athletic director came on board, he and I met to discuss the program and the future of baseball. Immediately, I could tell he was more interested in basketball, football, and revenues. I drove home that night knowing I wasn't going to be a good fit with the new boss. I resigned my position, even without having another job to fall back on. Luckily, I was hired as a high school athletic director one month later, but my seven years at Whitworth were over with the snap of my fingers. I chose to avoid what I anticipated would be a difficult relationship with the new athletic director. Given my dedication and commitment, when Whitworth hired a person I couldn't work with, it caused me to feel angry and betrayed. The new athletic director lasted only two years, and it took me over ten years to forgive the university I love so much for what had happened. When we forgive, we free a prisoner and the prisoner is us.

When dealing with things we don't like or people we don't care for, Washington State Hall of Fame Football Coach Ed Fisher would say, "You're going to get over it, you might as well get over it sooner than later" (E. Fisher, personal communication, 2002). However, forgiving is hard, and it often takes time. In "Forgiveness Can Improve Mental and Physical Health" (Weir, 2017) states, "Many people think of forgiveness as letting go or moving on. But there's more to it than that. True forgiveness goes a step further, offering something positive – empathy, compassion, understanding – toward the person who hurt you." There is no reason to hold a grudge. When we hold onto our anger toward others, it makes it difficult to rebuild that relationship or for it to be productive. I've held grudges against others, where I have refused to forgive the other person or move on after a dispute. Likely, you have experienced this as well. What good has this done either of us? Nothing. My advice is to forgive and forget. We need to let go of our grudges against our families, friends, staff members, other people, or another company. Those grudges act like an anchor – holding us back on our forward progress.

The "Reset" Button

There are opportunities where we can hit the "reset" button on our relationships. When we hit the reset button, we can slow down, reflect, and reset with a person or a situation. Although there are no do-overs in life, there are certainly opportunities and situations where the reset button can help us, especially when both parties are willing to address the reasons the relationship needed to be reset in the first place.

An example of when our entire country was able to reset occurred on September 11, 2001. It was a heartbreaking and devastating incident which hit close to home for all Americans. Following the terrorist attacks that occurred that day, Americans from all walks of life came together to support one another. The love for our country overcame individual differences. Even those that were not directly impacted by this event were able to reset their thinking. We held our families and friends closer than ever, and we all realized that life could end in an instant and we needed to value the time that we have in our lives. Life is too short to hold grudges, to hold onto needless anger – to not spend all of our minutes together in positive interactions.

The financial crisis of 2007 - 2008 affected our nation in a way that has only happened a couple of times in the history of the stock market. During this time, people had to come together to support one another. It was difficult for many people to overcome losing their homes and their jobs. Unemployment and homelessness was high, and community members had to support people in crisis. Relationships helped families to survive this crisis. Friends created space in their basements to house those in need; people volunteered at food banks; teachers provided stability for kids. Without key relationships, many more people would have lost their way during this time.

Most recently, the quarantine orders the U.S. experienced during spring and summer of 2020 has led for many to reset their lives. This unavoidable "slowdown" of busy lives has helped some families to reconnect in ways that never would have been possible. Albeit, being stuck at home for months on end in homes where relationships aren't strong could lead to a reset and result in stronger relationships or could lead to an even bigger breakdown of the relationships in question. Because of the risk of death across the nation and across the globe, COVID-19 paralyzed people in a way never seen before. Our lives that were going at high speed in March 2020 were suddenly paused. We worked to maintain connections with people outside our homes, and this time was especially hard for those living alone. During the Coronavirus, things looked much different in my home: homework looked different, work looked different and family dinners came back to life. Although difficult, our time together was also refreshing and the reset button was not only important, it was necessary.

Each of these three events impacted people and some were able to hit a reset button and make the best out of these inevitable experiences. These events provided an opportunity for people to slow down and reconnect. People were either in shock and fear, were laid off from work, worked from home, or had to change the way they normally did things, and these factors forced people to reset their lives to meet the new demands after the crisis. In some cases, families dealt with the impact of death and devastation. After a national crisis, those people who got back up and tried again – to mend their lives and their relationships – are the ones who can show the rest of us how to be strong and how to reset.

The reset button provides an opportunity for people to catch their breath, reset and re-center themselves, and do things differently. Some people are looking for the "easy" button. There isn't an easy button in life. No one gets to magically push a button to make it easier, not for ourselves, our family, or our organization. I would rather have a reset button than an easy button. At least when we reset, we are able to try again and learn from our mistakes. The hard work it takes to reset our relationships is worth it in the end because when the hard work pays off, the reward is even sweeter.

Growing Your Relationships

Reflecting on the upside, downside, and beliefs related to relationships will help one to be more aware of what goes into a relationship and what they can gain from having strong relationships with others. I developed the following guidelines to help grow our relationships:

1. Self-Awareness - know what our strengths and weaknesses are in our relationships

2. Self-Improvement - make a commitment to grow in our ability to develop relationships

3. Self-Actualization - see ourselves and others growing in our relationships

4. Self-Responsibility - acknowledge I am responsible for my attitude and actions

These four guidelines will help you to assess each of your relationships and determine where you need to work on making them stronger. During Chapter 2 and 3, I discussed characteristics of strong relationships, including caring, kindness, quality time, trust, and communication. How will you address these elements in your current relationships? Use Figure 4.2 to plan for your own relationships (see Figure 4.2).

Figure 4.2

Action Plan: Relationships II

Who do you have the strongest relationships with? Why?
1.
2.
Which characteristics from Chapter 2 and 3 do these relationships demonstrate?
1.
2.
Describe a relationship in your life that could be stronger. What are some steps you can take to improve this relationship?
Which of the elements that impact relationships do you plan to work on going forward?

Note: Use this action plan to analyze your relationships using information from Chapters 2 and 3.

Use this action plan to analyze your personal relationships. Focus specifically on kinship, friendship, and mentorship.

Chapter 5: Leader*Ship*

"It's a lot easier to criticize a leader than to be one."

(T. Whitaker, personal communication, April 27, 2020)

Most people don't want to lead. That is not who we are. There have been times when we didn't want to lead, and we still did it anyway. I am a leader and so are you. Sometimes we will be a leader by default, and other times because we really wanted to be the leader. Either way, leading isn't easy. In fact, it can be very difficult. There are times when we have said to ourselves, "I would love to hand this off - this decision, the pressure, the responsibility - to someone else." Admit it because it is true. But, we aren't going to hand off the decisions and the responsibility to someone else. Leading is difficult and it is also gratifying because, as leaders, we know our leadership will make a difference. We know there are people who are counting on our leadership.

If leading was easy, everyone would choose to lead. Yet, everyone is leading. Everyone has the ability to influence, help, and support others. As leaders, we won't opt out of leading. We are going to opt into leading. Our family needs us, our spouse needs us, and our children need us. Our team needs us and so does our company or organization. It won't be easy and the difficulty is what makes it great. So, let's rise up and lead.

Leadership is the ability to help others work together for a common purpose. Leadership is also about knowing when to lead from the front, from the middle, and from the back. In order to be an effective leader, one must be able to lead from all three. Leaders are the equalizer for their family, team, and organization. In this chapter, we will consider the various characteristics of leadership that are necessary for leaders to develop. These characteristics include understanding the role in leadership, including being able to lead from the front, middle, and back of the fleet; having a clear vision for the team; developing a focus on service to our team and community; experience discomfort to benefit the team; and a willingness to continue to adapt and learn.

Why Do I Lead?

"Why do I lead?" This is the question every effective leader must know and be able to explain to others. We must know our "Why" – it is our driving purpose. The question is simple, but the answer is not. There are so many reasons why I choose to lead. My top reasons to lead are simple:

- I want to help as many people as I can.

- I want to know I'm making a difference for other people.

- I enjoy seeing other people be successful.

When we know our reasons for leading, we become extremely clear in our purpose. We also begin to identify how we can make a difference in the lives of others. I encourage you to take the time to ask yourself: "Why am I leading?" Write the answers down using Figure 5.1 (see Figure 5.1) and cement these answers in your head and heart.

Figure 5.1

Why do I lead?

Identify the reasons you lead. What is your driving purpose? Put a star next to your top reasons.	

Note: Use these questions to identify the reasons you lead.

There are going to be times when you question your own leadership and whether you should be leading. Once you've written down your reasons, you will be reminded of your purpose for leading.

Every great leader I know is fascinated by the processes of leadership. Nearly every follower is obsessed with outcomes. This may be the defining factor between a successful leader and an unsuccessful one. Outcomes are one-time events; processes are repeated. Our processes can't be faked. Our families, our teams, our businesses, and our lives are defined by the processes we choose.

Developing a Clear Vision

Developing a clear vision requires the leader to take the time to think through and create a picture of how things will look, whether it is for one day, one month, one year, or a lifetime. Beginning with a destination first allows us to create this vision. A vision for ourselves as individual leaders is great; however, a vision for the family, staff, or organization requires having the entire team involved. Before we are able to create this vision, we must really know the people on our team.

Once we know "our people" really well, then we can focus on our vision. Our vision should include creating the culture we want. People can feel the culture of their team and the culture supported by the leadership; they can see it in actions and reactions; they can hear it as we communicate with them; and they can talk about it with each other. The leader's influence on their team helps everyone develop the desired culture. To develop a clear vision, there are several factors I suggest. Those will be discussed in the sections that follow. First, we will discuss leadership style.

Leaders Develop a Leadership Style

Developing a leadership style is a part of our leadership that evolves with time. As we take on a leadership role, we will likely begin to pay attention to other leaders and how they address and respond to certain situations. We might begin to admire certain styles and learn that we'd like to avoid others. Our leadership philosophy, discussed in the next section, may also influence the leadership style we wish to adopt. Eventually, all leaders develop a preferred leadership style that they rely on. According to Martinuzzi (2019), there are seven traditional types of Leadership Styles:

- Autocratic leadership.
- Charismatic leadership.
- Transformational leadership.
- Laissez-faire leadership.
- Transactional leadership.
- Supportive leadership.
- Democratic leadership.

The best leaders I've seen and been around, however, tend to use multiple leadership styles, depending on the situation. Being able to remain flexible to the situation is called *Situational Leadership* (Hersey & Blanchard, 1982). There will be times when we have to move from one leadership style to another, even in the same situation or on the same day.

Not only does one's leadership style often adapt to the situation, it also evolves as the leader changes and grows. Our experiences, our wisdom, our decisions, our teams - all will help influence our leadership style. Successful leaders are flexible. This flexibility allows us to adapt to ever changing circumstances. As we continue to fine-tune our leadership style over time, we will analyze and identify the important elements of our leadership style constantly.

Leaders Establish a Leadership Philosophy

Developing a leadership philosophy is an important decision every leader must make before they lead other people. What is your leadership philosophy? Whether you already have a leadership philosophy or not, I suggest considering the following to either develop or reflect on your leadership philosophy:

- Leaders see the very best in people.

- Leaders serve others.

- Leaders lead through strengths and see challenges as opportunities.

- Leaders make the very best decisions they can at the time of the situation and circumstances with the information they have.

- Leaders have the ability to adapt to a changing environment

These statements can help to guide our philosophy and build on the relationships and environment we hope to create on our team. Leaders must be able to find each person's niche on the team, and work to develop skills in that person. Being able to develop our team's skills, as well as learning and adapting to situations, will be discussed later in this chapter. These are key characteristics of leadership and should be included in our philosophy.

My leadership philosophy evolved from experiences, by reading about and researching other leaders' work, and through trial and error. Any philosophy draws on experience, learning, and research. These factors often influence how one approaches creating the philosophy. For some, the philosophy might be as short as a few sentences included in a mission or vision statement; for others, a philosophy takes pages and pages to explain. One thing is for certain: philosophies of teaching, behavior management, leadership, or myriad of other subjects are constantly evolving.

My leadership statement from five years ago is much different than the statement I have now – or what I will have five years in the future. When I began as an educator, I had some ideals that were quickly challenged when I started working with real students and colleagues. I had to adjust my philosophy to reflect what I learned that worked and didn't work in the classroom. As I honed my leadership style, I learned what works and what doesn't work for me and my personal style, as well.

Leaders Set Priorities

When developing a clear vision, leaders know how to keep focused. They don't get distracted by "shiny objects" or taken off-course by something flashy (Alvy, 2017). When we know what is most important we will be able to answer these questions: What are our most important priorities? Where is our focus? and Where is the focus for our team?

Stephen Covey, the author of *The 7 Habits of Highly Effective People* (1989), wrote about "Habit 3 – Put First Things First." This habit is about setting priorities. As you prioritize a) your important, b) not important, c) urgent, or d) non-urgent activities and responsibilities are, you become much clearer at setting your priorities. In Figure 5.2, you should think about your current "to do" list (see Figure 5.2). Which of these items are important, not important, urgent, or non-urgent? You might also consider the length of time each task will take and plan accordingly.

Figure 5.2

Prioritizing

Activity or Responsibility	Priority level: important, not important, urgent, or non-urgent	Estimated time needed to complete
1.		
2.		
3.		
4.		
5.		
6.		
7.		
8.		
9.		
10.		

Note: This figure asks leaders to prioritize their activities and responsibilities in order to determine which is important, not important, urgent, and non-urgent.

This figure only includes room to rate ten items although some of us might have many more than ten things on our "to do" list. If that is the case, I recommend focusing on a smaller period of time and what needs to get done within the next week or two, and this should help focus the response. If long-term items need to be worked on in the next week or two, include those, as well. When we focus on priorities, we keep the focus on our vision, and we are less susceptible to distractions.

Leaders Establish Clear Expectations

Clear expectations allow leaders to determine what they expect from themselves and their team. A parent, who is the leader of the family, decides what they expect from their family, such as expectations for children to take care of their room, pet, and chores/responsibilities; for driving the car; for dating responsibly; for keeping up at school; or for participating in extracurricular activities. A coach, who is the leader of a sports or work team, decides on expectations for their athletes and team members by establishing norms and expectations. An administrator decides what teachers and staff at the school are expected to do in their job duties. Without a set of clear expectations, it's difficult for those following a leader to see a clear path; it's like going on a road trip without a map.

The structure of the organization must be centered on the question: "What is expected of me to do well?" It is important at all times, regardless of the leadership position we hold, to communicate clear expectations to all parties involved. As mentioned in Chapter three (pp. 29-33), being able to communicate effectively with our team is essential for developing strong relationships, and without clear communication of expectations, our relationships with our team will suffer – and as a result, our leadership will also suffer. These clear expectations are important for everybody involved in the organization; the values, standards, and rules of the leader, when consistent, will be the values, standards, and rules for the organization.

In order to be consistent, a leader must have a clear set of values, standards, and rules for employees and the organization itself. Consistency brings order to our family, team, or organization. As the leader, we assist and support team members so they regularly achieve objectives and improve overall performance. When a leader is consistent, they are able to inspire trust. The structure of having clear expectations ensures everyone knows exactly what is expected. These expectations create a clear path toward the outcome we want our team or organization to achieve. People admire and respect consistent leadership. When the leader is being inconsistent, mixed messages are sent that confuse people. As a leader, we won't necessarily treat everyone the same: however, we can be consistent and treat everyone with the same expectations that apply to all involved in the organization. Organizational expectations help leaders to know what is expected at every single level of the organization and are critical for everyone who works in the organization. Have you developed your expectations for employment?

Everywhere I have worked, I have worked with my team to develop expectations for employment. We are very clear with these and the expectations are non-negotiable. What do we expect of our school district employees? The Freeman School District is committed to the following expectations for employment:

1. Be nice – be nice and treat all students, staff, and parents with respect at all times.

2. The 5 R's – Relationships, Rigor, Relevance, Results, and Rewards.

3. "Kaizen" – continuous improvement individually and as a team member.

4. Teamwork – a total team player who works well within a process driven organization.

5. The Washington State Professional Code of Conduct. (Freeman School District, 2013)

The expectations for employees vary depending on the context of the organization. The Freeman School District Employee Expectations clearly identify the people we serve and work with as a number one priority. The five expectations included in this list also demonstrate a focus on *The 3 Ships*; relationships, leadership, and partnerships are a strong focus of the expectations for our district employees.

Leaders Expand Their Field of Vision

Looking through a telescope or into a microscope provides us with a much different view of the world. The lens we look through impacts what we see, and our experiences influence the type of lens we see through. Leaders must learn to look through the lenses their stakeholders see through even when the lens is different from the one we typically see through. For example, I remember learning in English class to examine texts for bias, to consider different viewpoints, to look for whose voice was missing in a text, and even to read using questions that helped develop critical thinking. Each of these helped me to practice using a different lens to think about the text. I wasn't expected to read it simply to enjoy it, even though I sometimes did; rather, I read it with the purpose of looking for these other items. My English teacher provided me with the lens to use and helped me to practice the type of thinking I would need to use regularly in my leadership role as an adult. Leaders have to think about how people from a different background might feel about our vision, how people from a different culture might interpret it, what assumptions we've made about the people in our organization, and many other complicated factors that influence people who are impacted by the vision statement.

Leaders constantly expand their knowledge and perspective through their reflection, their thinking, their reading, their writing, their speaking, and their experiences which all build lenses to lead through. As we expand our knowledge and perspective, our field of vision expands. When we are driving a vehicle, we need our rearview mirror, side mirror, and the windshield. Even though the majority of our time is spent looking ahead through the windshield, we must also be able to use our rearview and side mirrors to help navigate our journey. Every once in a while we must reverse, in order to move forward again. This might happen when we discover what we think or believe may not actually be true. When this happens, we learn to look at something through a new lens, or perspective.

Knowing where we have been, where we are, and where we are going helps expand our field of vision. It also helps us understand life isn't an experience, life is a series of experiences. Leaders know life requires us to know when to batten down the hatches, pull anchor to float, change course, and abandon ship. Our crew is not always ready at the same time so we must be willing to meet them where they are. Expanding our field of vision will help us, and others, navigate everything life throws at us.

Leaders Have One Eye on Today and One Eye on Tomorrow. Leaders must balance the need to have one eye on today and one eye on tomorrow, while still remembering the past and its lessons. In order to develop a clear vision for the organization, leaders must have institutional memory, as well as have a plan for moving the organization forward. The vision we have for our team and organization should include short and long-term goals. These are like driving on a highway; we look in the rearview mirror, experience the road underneath us, and also look forward to anticipate what's coming up.

Being able to have a big picture in mind is a skill leaders have to develop. Decisions that are made in the organization have ripple effects, and leaders must anticipate what those ripples might be. Like the example of repairing a car (see Chapter 2), certain decisions will impact what happens next. We might be able to repair the car with a piece of duct tape, but the organization may be better off in the future with an investment in a proper repair. So many factors impact the difficult decisions leaders must make, and great leadership almost requires being able to predict the future

– or at least to anticipate it. For example, leaders face many difficult decisions during recessions (i.e. the Great Recession of 2008 or the COVID-19 Pandemic of 2020). Cuts to faculty and staff were made in education, and the uncertainty of how long it would take for the economy to recover and how these events would impact society made these cuts scary for leaders. Many had to consider the health of the organization over individual employees. This example attempts to describe the complexity of looking at the past, present, and future at the same time.

Successful leaders have a toolbox. This toolbox holds the different tools we need to help lead our team. Our toolbox increases in size through time and experience. Learning how to use the correct tools allows the leader to be an effective leader and problem solver. When looking at the present and future, leaders use a telescope and microscope. Thinking about today and the future at the same time means being able to look both up close and far into the distance, and having a telescope and a microscope allows the leader to be prepared for both.

Leaders Align Their Focus on Serving and Developing People. People follow people they believe in, and by developing a clear vision for our organizations we demonstrate our ability to serve and develop our team. As leaders develop a vision, I suggest asking the following questions:

- How does this vision support a people-centered focus?

- Does this vision consider the needs of stakeholders?

- How does this vision serve people?

- How does this vision develop relationships, leadership, and partnerships with the family, team or company?

- What opportunities are there for stakeholders to grow in the organization?

Having an eye on the future means that we might have our eye on particular people within our organization that could take on future leadership roles. But, in order for that to happen, we need to prepare them for those future roles.

When people within our organization know they have the opportunity to grow within the organization, many are more motivated to support the vision of the leader. Getting buy-in from our team is essential, and one way to do this is to develop those people into leaders. For example, Chuck Stocker, retired Superintendent from the Freeman (WA) School District, always poses questions and situations for me. Chuck challenges me to think about things I may not have considered. His experience provides me with a new lens from which to look. Why does Chuck help me and the Freeman team? As a former leader of the Freeman District, he is still an important stakeholder – he provides me with the institutional memory I need as I make decisions. He expands my leadership skills and prepares me, and the team, for the future when he poses difficult questions. This has been a constant process for almost ten years, and Chuck has ingrained in my mind the need to always ask the difficult questions. I like to ask the what-if questions to our team. One question I pose to my own team is, "What should we be thinking about that no one else is thinking about?" This helps us prepare for the what-ifs and our future.

Why should you do the same thing for your team as Chuck does for me? The answer is simple - leaders serve their team and develop the next generation of leaders. When we lead discussions about the future of the organization and pose difficult questions, we are preparing them for whatever comes their way in the future. Engage the team to think about things no one else is thinking about. Prepare the team so when someone leaves, the team doesn't miss a beat regardless of the situation. A sign of a great organization is the ability to adapt; the team continues to operate at the same level of efficiency or effectiveness regardless of the configuration of the team itself.

Leaders Adapt Their Vision to a Changing Environment. Leadership is about helping and leading others to be their very best for a greater cause than the individual. Leadership deals with people and their dynamics, which are continually changing. The challenge of leadership is to adapt to change while facilitating growth.

Every organization is a living organization. Things change constantly, and the one thing we can count on as a leader is change. We will have control over some of these changes, but we won't be able to control many things that change, including the changing environment around us. As a leader, we can choose to either embrace or resist change; however, change is inevitable. And, the most effective leaders adapt to a changing environment. If we are leading correctly, then our team will change. We will either help people grow up in the organization (i.e. a promotion, more responsibility) or grow out of the organization (i.e. retirement, a promotion with another company). Every time our family, team, or organization has a change, then we must help our team adapt to this change. We have a saying in Freeman: "New Player...New Team."

We can learn from the past, but we can't live there. Our vision must include a clear strategy with our team that plans to adapt to the changing environment. If we need some motivation, take a look at the history of Blockbuster, Kodak, and Pan-Am, to name a few. These companies weren't able to adapt to a changing environment. By the time they made the decisions to change, it was too late. Looking at these companies reminds us that we are either improving or we aren't improving – there is no middle ground. As leaders, we will not only be helping ourselves, but also the team, to prepare for the future by adapting to the changing environment. At the same time, we are also helping everyone see and build a path forward.

Leaders Get Out of Their Comfort Zone. A "comfort zone" is the behavioral space where activities and behaviors fit a routine and pattern that minimizes stress and risk. It provides a state of mental security. Staying in the comfort zone benefits people in obvious ways: regular happiness, low anxiety, and reduced stress. Getting out of the comfort zone is exciting for some while it might be terrifying for others. Excellent leaders encourage not only themselves, but their entire team to step out of the comfort zone in order to take on new projects or strategic plans. These leaders take the people on their team places they need to go even when they don't know it.

There are many ways to move out of the comfort zone. In order to take someone to a new place, the leader must first be willing to go to a new place. As we get out of our comfort zone, we will take risks and have failures. We can try a new strategy, go someplace we haven't been, explore a new viewpoint, or change the familiar routine to include a new activity. We can move our team from their comfort zones in small doses, and when we model it ourselves, we take others with us. People in the organization (i.e. ourselves, team members, stakeholders) want to take a few small risks, and as a result, learn from the challenges in order to learn new approaches. Without moving out of the comfort zone, teams cannot grow. It is necessary to try new activities and behaviors in order to move toward the goals and vision of the organization; otherwise, the team would be stagnant. Moving out of the comfort zone allows stretching, growth, and expansion.

Leaders Know Success Builds Confidence, But Failure Builds Character. We learn more from our failures than our successes. Many people gauge success by how we react to our failures. Most of the time we get it right when responding to our failures, though sometimes we don't. We pride ourselves as leaders who wants to be a positive, collaborative, and problem solvers. We want to be team players. Ultimately, we want to make the very best decisions we can to support and serve the people we are leading. No matter what, we must continue working together to find solutions, even as we sometimes need to fail forward to achieve success in the long run.

No leader, family, team, company, or governing body is going to be perfect. Leaders claim their failures and admit their mistakes. We are going to make mistakes and it is okay to make mistakes. We can and should learn from our mistakes. The traditional saying, "It's important to try different things. It's better to have tried and failed, than to have never tried at all" comes to mind. I remember hearing this while growing up, playing baseball, trying new things at work, and to this day when something new comes up. We all can fail forward as long as we keep our eye on serving and take care of the people who matter to us most: our family, friends, team, company and customers.

Service to the Team

When the leader stays focused on serving his/her/their team, then an important message is sent. This message is: "I'm here to serve my team first, not myself." If a family knows the leader is more interested in serving others before the leader's own interests, then family members know the leader's actions and decisions are in the best interest of the group. This unselfish approach is often called servant leadership. As leaders, we are here to provide service to our teams, and I believe if I help and serve others first, then I will be helped and served as well.

There are two ways to improve our team - improve the staff we have or get better staff. We improve our staff and leadership team members by providing opportunities for them to grow and develop their leadership skills and influence within the organization. We improve our team by offering high-quality professional development. We also improve our team by hiring someone better than the person they replaced. This is the goal every time we have a job opening. At Freeman, we use the saying, "Good hires prevent forest fires." When the leader stays focused on serving and developing their team, their team will serve and develop the leader.

Things in life rise and fall: bread in the oven, the stock market, the water level of lakes and rivers. Leadership rises and falls, as well. John C. Maxwell one of the world's most renowned experts on leadership stated, "Everything rises and falls with leadership" (2011). If we want to make a positive impact on the world, then learning to lead better will help us do it, and one of the most important concepts to remember about leadership is that it is about serving other people - it isn't about serving ourselves. As long as we focus on helping as many people as we can, we will know our leadership is making a difference.

Leadership is Influence

Influence is a key component in leadership. Leaders have the ability to influence others, and sometimes they may not even know the power they have to influence a particular person. Though their influence, leaders shape the direction, decisions, and development of their teams and organizations. Vocabulary.com defines influence as:

...the power to have an important effect on someone or something. If someone influences someone else, they are changing a person or thing in an indirect but important way. Sometimes a person who influences another doesn't intend to have any effect, but sometimes they are using influence to benefit themselves. (Vocabulary.com, n.d.)

This definition captures some of the intricacies of influence. Our influence as leaders applies to our ability to influence individuals, families, companies, and organizations, even national governments. To influence leaders must have access. To have access requires credibility and the leader must be known for the credibility of their information. In particular, in service-oriented fields like education, all faculty, staff, and administrators must consider the power we have to influence others. Our role as an influencer should never be abused, but if people can increase their influence with others, they can lead more effectively.

SHAPE. Before we are able to influence others, we must first know them. During Chapters two, three, and four, we discussed the importance of developing relationships. Effective leaders must have strong relationships with members of their team. And, those relationships must come first. Without those strong connections, we will struggle to lead.

The Way of the Shepherd (Leman & Pentak, 2004) discusses the SHAPE (Strengths, Heart, Attitude, Personality, and Experiences) of the flock. The flock can be comprised of family, team members, the organization, or anyone else in the leader's care. Before we can lead them, before we are able to influence them, we must know their SHAPE. We must learn about them as people first, then as valued team members, before we can lead them. Ask yourself: Do I know personal facts about every person I lead? Their families, their interests, their hobbies? What do I know about them as people? Use Figure 5.3 to formulate additional questions you could use to learn about your team (see Figure 5.3).

Figure 5.3

Developing SHAPE with My Team

What questions could you ask to discover more about your team by using the SHAPE strategy?	
Strengths	Sample: What is this person good at
Heart	Sample: What do I know about this person's family?
Attitude	Sample: How does this person react when he/she/they make a mistake?
Personality	Sample: What is this person's hobbies outside of work?
Experiences	Sample: Where has this person worked before?

Note. This figure includes the SHAPE strategy and some sample questions for leaders to consider when developing SHAPE with their team.

Each of the questions you develop and work to answer with people on your team will build a stronger relationship with that person. Building a strong relationship is the first step toward being able to influence your team.

Leaders Are the Filter. Leaders are like an air filter. We allow good air to pass through, and we block anything that can cause damage. People share more information when they feel they can trust the leader or when they feel the leader can help them. The leader has to be able to determine the important information, from the unimportant. The valid complaints, from those that are not. This information is often used to provide feedback to the team member, to provide constructive guidance, and to determine ways to improve. The leader must use a filter to determine how to approach each employee, and this filter is often created through the knowledge the leader has of each employee.

Leaders also use different sized filters, depending on the situation. When we have a fragile employee, then the leader may use a thicker filter. With most people, the leader uses the regular sized filter. With some people, the leader can also use no filter. Each situation and each person requires the leader to use their skills in determining, what size, if any, filter is needed.

Leaders Develop Positive Teams

Successful leaders believe positive teams create a positive culture. This, in turn, leads to a positive experience for customers, employees, and organizations. Jon Gordon writes in *The Power of a Positive Team* that positive teams:

1. Create positive cultures

2. Work together toward a shared vision with a greater purpose

3. Work together with optimism, positivity, and belief

4. Transform and remove negativity

5. Communicate and connect

6. Commit and care

7. Are always striving to get better (Gordon, 2018)

These are key characteristics to developing a positive team and, in result, a positive culture in our organization. The culture of the organization often determines how willing people are to go out of their way to help one another. Building a positive culture must start with a positive leader. How the leader reacts - to adversity, a bad day, a crisis – shows the team how they should react. A supportive, positive culture also contributes to job satisfaction. The shared vision and purpose impacts the team's attitude. Frustration over an unclear vision or unclear expectations can doom a team. When the team has clear expectations and a clear vision, they can remain optimistic and positive because they believe their organization can get through any difficulties.

This changes problems into prospects. It transforms challenges into opportunities. The team doesn't adopt a deficit viewpoint; rather, they see the strengths each team member, and the organization, brings to each new dilemma. A positive team also makes connections with one another – and not only at work. Team members genuinely care for one another, and a great leader works to align personalities and hire people that will compliment other people's strengths. People are more willing to work through challenges in an organization if they belong to a team they genuinely feel connected to.

One of my mentors, Harry Amend (see Chapter 4), focused his efforts on developing people through a positive team approach. His $2 + 2 = 5$ equation (H. Amend, personal communication, 1996) shows when people work together the outcome is greater than the sum of its parts. This equation demonstrates the foundation for building relationships by developing trust in and between team members. He treated everyone the same to a point, and then he didn't. He knew how to connect with people at their level. Individuals and teams who add value to each other and to the entire team provide the organization with a double win. A double win helps put chips in our stack and helps us develop a positive team.

As leaders, we are going to deal with both positivity and negativity within our organization. Some questions to consider include:

- How do you deal with positivity and negativity on your team?

- How does positivity or negativity impact the team culture?

- How do you work toward buy-in from all team members?

- How do you model appropriate norms that reflect the culture you want to develop?

- Are you going to make decisions based on your positive team members?

- How are you going to deal with the "squeaky wheels" in your company?

Ultimately, the more positive we are as a leader, the more positive our teams will be and the better chance our culture will be positive.

Leaders Enhance a "Customer Service" Approach

In leadership, customer service refers not only to the people being served by the organization, but also those within the organization that we serve through our leadership. Throughout this section, I chose to refer to service in both realms as customer service, because I view my employees, my teachers, my staff, my students, and my students' parents all as my "customers." If I don't serve them, then I am not meeting my expectations as a person, teacher, administrator, or leader.

Leaders focus on great customer service. What is the difference between poor, okay, good, or great customer service? My answer is simple: satisfaction and loyalty. When customers aren't satisfied, it's likely related to how they were treated. It's not what happened, it is how it happened. There are different levels of customer satisfaction, and when customers are satisfied, they feel like they received good customer service. When a customer feels satisfaction, they become loyal to the company. When this occurs, we know we have great customer service.

Dr. Gary Livingston was the master of customer service. Gary created an atmosphere of trust through his communication and customer service to the people he served with. When I was hired as a new administrator and met Gary for the first time, he made a comment I will never forget: "Randy, tell me what I can do to help you be successful." Gary was most interested in how to help me and support my development: talk about customer service and making me feel valued!

As the leader, our customer service approach to our team and with those we serve will become the gold standard for our company. Everyone wants excellent customer service and this starts with us. Treat others the way we want to be treated, and we will like the results our customers will receive from our company. Customer service should be an important part of our vision.

Leaders Believe in the 95% Rule

When considering the needs of the team, leaders must make decisions based on the majority. Ask yourself: Will this decision benefit most of my team or only a few? Leaders have to weigh the cost of decisions and try to make choices that will benefit the most team members while trying to meet the needs of the organization and the established vision.

Harry Amend taught me the 95% Rule. This piece of his *Ten Tools for Success* (H. Amend, personal communication, 1996) states a leader, "will not make statements, decisions, or rules based on what is going on with only 5% of [the] team." Harry believes 95% of customers, employees, and leaders will do, say, and lead in the right way. The challenge for leaders, then, and a true sign of our leadership, is how we deal with the other 5% who don't follow the rules, don't meet the expectations, fail to support the vision of the organization, and seem to constantly need our attention, time, and resources. This means 5% of the members of our team cannot make the other 95% suffer for their mistakes. Leaders need to address the outliers, the other 5%, one-on-one. This requires crucial, difficult conversations with a small group of employees.

The 95% Rule can be applied to any group whether it is children, adults, acquaintances, or team members. Leaders can't allow a small handful of people to take away from the fact a large number of stakeholders are doing the right thing. They are doing things correctly. When we need to deal with the 5%, remember to praise in public and criticize or coach in private.

Continuing to Learn

On a personal and professional level, we always have opportunities to grow and learn. As a life-long learner, I learn something new every day. On a personal level, my continuous learning is about expanding my skills to increase my knowledge. On a professional level, continuously learning is about developing skills so I may be a better leader to respond to new developments and a changing environment.

Leaders Focus on "Kaizen"

"Kaizen" is Japanese for improvement, or change for the better, which refers to the philosophy or practices focused upon continuous improvement of processes (Vocabulary.com, n.d.). When the leader is focused on continuous improvement – for our family, students, staff, team, and entire organization – then there is an opportunity for growth. Important components of kaizen are developing processes, continually getting out of the comfort zone, and helping others get out of their comfort zones. Asking tough questions about where we are, where we want to be, and how we plan to get there strengthens relationships by creating trust through candid and caring conversations.

When leaders think they have "arrived," then they are done as a leader. When leaders think they have all the answers, then their team will stop following them. When leaders believe "me" is better than "we," they will have a one-person team. They will be walking alone and no one will be beside them; their team will be behind or even in front of them – not with them. Those leaders' teams will be gone because leaders who cannot strive for constant improvement are not reflective or effective at their job. There is always room for improvement and kaizen starts with improving the leader before improving the team.

Leaders Listen, Learn, Lead, and then Reflect

Listening is a lost art. Most people are so interested in sharing their thoughts and ideas, they aren't listening to or thinking about what the other person is saying. As leaders, we must listen, learn, and then lead. Listening first allows us to gather better information. Including voices from the team in our decisions creates leadership based on the interests and needs of those on our team. There are multiple ways for us to learn.

My first suggestion is to lead with listening, asking great questions, learning as much as we can and then leading. For example, on my team, everyone gets their say, but not everyone gets their way. This allows for an environment where people feel safe. They can share their ideas, suggestions, and thoughts openly, without fear. Team members are able to focus on what is being said and not who is saying it; ask as many questions as necessary; and know they're going to be able to share their opinions. It also means not always getting our way. There are times when, as the leader, I don't get what I want. Here are the steps I use for promoting "listen, learn, and lead":

1. Listen intently

2. Ask great questions

3. Focus on *what* not *whom*

4. Learn as much as one possibly can

5. Lead

I suggest leaders use these five steps to develop better listening within their team. As always, leaders need to start with themselves and model excellent listening behavior so that team members learn to adopt those norms in their interactions with others on the team, as well. By listening effectively, the team learns from one another and more ideas are shared and spread.

After "listen, learn, and lead," I recommend reflection. Dr. Gene Sharratt says, "Learning does not occur during the act itself, learning occurs upon reflecting upon the act" (G. Sharratt, personal communication, 2020). While we experience things, we are too caught up in the moment to think about what we learned in the situation; instead, we learn best when we think about what happened later. When I reflect on a previous experience, I ask myself the following questions: (1) What went well? (2) What didn't go so well? (3) What should we have done differently? (4) What should I have done differently? and (5) If I was in a similar position again, how would I do things next time? These questions help me to focus on how the experience can be used in a positive way. I ask myself these questions after both good and bad experiences because I always strive for improvement.

Once the leader has trained themselves on these steps (listen, learn, lead, and reflection), they will be able to apply these principles to their leadership regularly, and begin to take their leadership and team to the next level.

Leaders Practice Self Care

Leaders are so focused on taking care of other people that they often fail to care for themselves. Parents take care of their children; the leader takes care of their team; and at the end of the day, time runs out, and we just don't do a very good job of taking care of ourselves. Many leaders shortchange themselves of sleep, they don't utilize healthy eating habits or fitness routines, and they often try to manage their stress through alcohol or drugs. It's tempting to leaders to dedicate too much time to their work, but without a work-life balance, leaders run the risk of burn-out. If leaders aren't happy and healthy themselves, it will be difficult (or impossible) to care for others. Research regarding self-care details the importance of paying attention to one's own physical and mental health. Self-care is a big part of treatment for many physical and mental health disorders. In *"Self-Care: 4 Ways to Nourish Body and Soul,"* Tello (2017) discusses the importance and the benefits of focusing on physical activity, eating well, calming one's mind, and sleeping well.

Abraham Lincoln once said, "Give me six hours to chop down a tree and I will spend the first four sharpening the axe" (Anderson, 2012). While Lincoln may have been talking about spending time preparing for success, he also could have been referring to mental preparedness. Leaders need to be mentally prepared to lead, and for the past fifteen years I have been providing a professional development training/seminar called "Sharpening Your Saw... Taking Care of Yourself First" based on Stephen Covey's *7 Habits of Highly Effective People,* habit number 7 "Sharpen Your Saw" (1989). The focus of this habit is on taking care of yourself first, so you can then take care of others. In Figure 5.4, I share four ways to "Sharpen Your Saw" based on Covey's habit (see Figure 5.4).

Figure 5.4

Sharpening Your Saw

> 1. Physical well-being - being active and taking care of yourself through your walking, workouts and your nutrition and diet.
> 2. Mental well-being - taking care of your mind, your mental well-being and your mental health.
> 3. Social-Emotional well-being - building positive relationships, your connections, and how you work as a part of a team.
> 4. Spiritual well-being - this is not necessarily about religion. This is about your spiritual experiences and it certainly can be connected to your faith.

Note: This list was developed based on "Sharpen Your Saw" (Covey, 1989). When I conduct trainings based on this concept, I have used this list to focus the areas of well-being to focus on.

The training I facilitate helps leaders "Sharpen Their Saws." With "Sharpen Your Saw," participants become accountable to a partner and develop a pledge card committing to focus on three specific items that they can do immediately. Leaders practice self-care by taking care of themselves first – by "Sharpening Their Saws." Only by doing this, can leaders be at their very best and in turn, be able to help others be at their very best. Are you willing to commit to your self-care? How will you "Sharpen Your Saw"?

Leading Myself Before Leading Others

In a previous section "Developing a Clear Vision," I provided research and guidelines to help each leader decide on their leadership principles and values. Top leaders across the world lead with their principles and values, and each one of us must determine what is important. No one else can tell a leader what their principles and values will be. The leader must decide. When one really knows them self and know who they are, what they stand for, what is important, what they want to accomplish, and how to help others, then they are ready to lead others. Leading oneself better will help lead others better.

As leaders, we have both personal and professional accountabilities. Ultimately we are accountable to (1) ourselves first, (2) next, to our family, and (3) finally, to our organization or company. So many people have this order backwards. And, although these people may flourish at work, they will suffer with their own well-being and the well-being of their family. Believe me, I struggled because I had this accountability order transposed in my own life. It took me too long to figure out, but I did eventually figure it out; I now make time to take care of myself, and this has helped me to have energy to care for others that are important in my life.

Leaders Carry Their Own Weather System

It's amazing how much the weather can impact a person's mood. When it is sunny and warm outside, most people have a little extra bounce in their step. If it's cold outside - especially if it is rainy or cloudy - most people would rather find shelter, snuggle into a warm cup of coffee, and read a good book or watch a movie. Weather can also impact our leadership, and our weather system can positively or negatively influence our three ships. If our ship is out in open, calm waters, then the sailing is smooth. If our ship is in rocky waters or is taking on water, then our family, team, or organization will have difficulties as well.

Each person carries their own weather system. As the leader, our emotional weather system influences other people. So as a leader, we must find a way to lead with a sunny and warm disposition, even if we're experiencing a rainstorm, a tornado, or even a hurricane. Why? Because families, staff members and organizations adopt the weather system of their leader. This is why emotional well-being is such an integral part of "Sharpen Your Saw." Once people learn to control their emotions and care for themselves, it helps them to develop stronger leadership.

How Your Brain Processes Thoughts. In many ways our brains are like computers. What we input affects how the brain tells the rest of our body to act. For example, we know when we have fear, it releases a chemical in our body. This can push us into actions which can harm us, instead of pushing us to do things that will protect us. When this happens, we use our "lizard brain," which utilizes our fight or flight response.

We have control over our brain. The reticular activating system will work in our favor, but we must be disciplined. When negative thoughts come into our mind, if we allow them to stay, they will impact our body's chemicals. We can't lead ourselves, and we can't move forward to be a positive influence for our spouse, children, family, team, or company if we are unable to filter out the negative thoughts. In order to lead the right way, we must completely wipe away our fear and doubt. Negative thoughts are like a fog that won't be lifted until we decide not to let negative thoughts stay in our head.

As a leader, I have had experiences where I was afraid and had doubts in my head. One example was when I had to speak about the unthinkable - one of our students had been killed in one of our buildings during the school day during a school shooting. I was very nervous and anxious to speak in front of 3,000 community members and a livestream audience to tens of thousands of people. It was one of the most difficult things I've ever experienced. I turned to the heavens and asked for strength. Along with this strength and the support of my family and friends, I was able to push through it. I still think about the experience almost every day. But, I also think about how I was able to control my reticular activity in order to control the negative thoughts and the fog I was in.

Leaders must be disciplined to focus on the right things: the positive thoughts, images, and discussions which assure, motivate, and inspire others. There are opportunities to create a "switch" in our head where we can turn negative thoughts into positive ones.

How Your Thoughts Affect Your Actions. Once we learn how to control our thoughts, then we can better control our actions. Accepting our reality means being able to develop a game plan. We can sit down with our families, our teams, and our companies to make things better - even if it is a small step towards a better plan.

We need to step up and take action after developing our game plan. Leaders have people counting on action: the team we employ is looking at us, our family is looking at us. We probably have heard the traditional saying, "Take one day at a time." By stepping up every day and taking on the challenges we face, we can win the day. Then, we can do the same the next day, and win again. And so on and so forth. Soon we will have won a week, then a month, and then we are on our way.

How Your Actions Affect Your Feelings. After changing the way we think and act, feelings can be affected in a positive way. We stay focused. We will start to see anger subside, doubt fade away, and our sense of confidence returns. We become so focused on doing what we have to do, including self-care, so we can do what we want to do – care for others. The result of this is we can now weather many storms.

Leaders understand how their brain processes, how their thoughts affect their actions, and how actions affect their feelings. These steps will allow us to work through issues and concerns while focusing on our priorities. Leaders know we may not have control over what happens: however, we do have control over how we respond.

Conclusion

In this chapter you were able to learn and think about your leadership, purpose, style, philosophy, thoughts, and actions. Use Figure 5.5 to develop an action plan that will help you in your leadership pursuits (see Figure 5.5).

Figure 5.5

Action Plan: Leadership

What are your three takeaways from this section?
1.
2.
3.
What are two strategies you will use to improve your leadership skills and abilities?
1.
2.
What steps will you take now? (Action Step for Leadership)

Note: This action plan will help you to develop steps to for improving your leadership.

Each of the main sections discussed in this chapter takes readers through a process of thinking deeply about their leadership and service to others. The chapter also reminds readers that self-care is important, and that healthy teams depend on leaders who are healthy.

Chapter 6: Leadership Challenges

"Things turn out best for those who make the best
of the way things turn out."

John Wooden (Wooden, 2005)

Every leader will have leadership challenges. This is inevitable and no leader will escape from the reality of these challenges. With each challenge, the leader has an opportunity to try to lead by themselves or with their team. A leader can't simply manage their way through the challenges; they must lead through the challenges. Building on the previous chapter, the strategies that follow in Chapter 6 will help develop leadership skills to guide the leader and their team through leadership challenges.

The purpose of this chapter is to provide tips and guidelines to leaders when faced with difficulties and challenges. This chapter begins by sharing tips for leading in crisis and developing a new normal after a crisis. Leaders know they must be willing to do what others can't and won't do during a crisis. It is a true test of leadership. The chapter also discusses ways to address weaknesses in leadership through assessments, including self-assessments and assessments completed by the team. Only through honest, thorough feedback can leaders address weaknesses. Finally, the chapter discusses the need for leaders to always remain vigilant in their leadership – keeping both hands on the wheel at all times. This will help the organization to stay on track and enable the leader to react to crises when they occur. Each of the sections in this chapter build toward a leader's capacity to address challenges and crises head-on and succeed.

Crisis and Challenge

There are going to be crises and challenges in life. Crises and challenges reveal who we are, what we are all about, and what we are made of. How the leader responds to crises and challenges reveals personal fortitude and true leaders rise during difficult times. No matter what the crisis is, there are areas of focus for all leaders. Figure 6.1 shares a list of guidelines I have developed for leading in crisis (see Figure 6.1).

Figure 6.1

Leading in Crisis

1. Put people first - it's all about how you can help others, lift others, and serve others.
2. Turn to the experts - they can provide support for you and your team.
3. Lead with optimism and hope - You must stay positive and lead with optimism.
4. Remain flexible - this allows you and your team to adapt to the uncertainty of the challenge or the difficulty.
5. Work as a team - four heads are better than three and all of us are smarter than one of us.
6. Communicate the facts - be honest, transparent and explain the challenge you are faced with.
7. Share the plan - all stakeholders must know the plan moving forward.

Note: This figure shares guidelines developed by the author for leading in crisis.

If the leader takes these steps, they will lead themselves and their people through it.

Crises in leadership are common. Although people don't often share their challenges with other people, they assign meaning to these events, and the events themselves have a profound impact on those that experienced the trauma. Leaders understand this and help lead their people out of challenging times. As the captain of the three ships, we need to help our crew get our ship out of rough waters. During a crisis, focus is necessary because there are so many activities happening at once. Fears and concerns are at peak levels, and we can help our team by prioritizing. The focus must be on needs and not on wants.

We know life is filled with challenges and rewards. There are some things in our control and there are other things that are out of our control. By staying calm, maintaining a positive spirit and approach, and focusing on what we have control of, both the good and the bad can get better. We cannot manage our way out of a crisis; we have to lead our way out of a crisis.

We are never going to be the same after a crisis. There is a new normal and we must define our new reality. My good friend, Jeffrey Bell, says, "Never waste a crisis" (J. Bell, personal communication, September 14, 2017). Get creative in your thinking, be bold in your decisions, and take action to help you and your team work through the crisis. In Figure 6.2, I share some steps I've developed that leaders can take to reflect and then respond as they find their new normal (see Figure 6.2).

Figure 6.2

Your New Normal

Steps	Reflection
1. take time by yourself to review and reflect	
2. use positive self - talk.	
3. ask great questions like how are we going to help move our team from where we are to where we want to be?	
4. ask yourself what should I be doing?	
5. ask yourself what should we be doing?	
6. take action.	

Note: In this figure, take the time to reflect and respond to how this crisis has impacted you and your team.

There is wisdom which comes out of crisis. Leaders and their organizations will be stronger having dealt with crises and difficulties.

Leaders Understand What They Can and Can't Control. There are things leaders will be able to control and things they won't be able to control. The key for us is to know the difference. As a leader, we can control our attitude and our effort. We can't control all of our thoughts. We probably won't be able to control the situation. But, we can control what we focus on and how we respond. As we think about what we do have control over, what we don't have control over, what we focus on, and how we respond, we will be able to be clearer in our thinking and in our responses.

Leaders are Willing to Do What Others Won't Do. It's easy to lead when things are going well. It's also easy to get people to connect, communicate, and work together when things are going well. It's much more challenging when things don't go well. Excellent leaders are willing to do what others won't do, regardless of whether things are going well or not.

There are going to be storms. Everyone has to deal with storms. There is going to be difficulty for every leader. Doing the right thing isn't always doing the popular thing, especially if there is a storm. Career expert, author, and national radio host Ken Coleman recently shared a story about animal responses to storms. He said this about being a buffalo:

A true thing about nature is how different animals, even from the same species, respond to handling a storm. When a cow, bless the cows, sees a storm coming across the plains, or coming across the pasture, they act like most human beings. They try to outrun the storm, but the storm overtakes them. Because the storm is faster than they are, they will spend more time in the storm because they are trying to run away from the storm.

The buffalo, these crazy animals, they're out on the plains and they see the storm. They run into the storm. The Buffalo doesn't run away from the storm, they run into the storm. As a result, they get through the storm quicker. (Coleman, 2020)

Ask yourself: How am I going to act when a storm comes? Will I act like a cow or a buffalo? Will I run from the storm or run into the storm? Leaders are willing to do what others won't do, even if it means running into a storm.

Leaders Use Assessments

Assessment tools are readily available for leaders to assess their three ships. Leaders need to be able to recognize their weaknesses and work toward eliminating or overcoming certain weaknesses in order to be stronger leaders. In this section, I will discuss the "fatal flaw" and how assessments and honest feedback can help leaders to confront their flaw(s). I will also share information about self-assessments and the value self-assessment has to provide feedback to leaders who are interested in continuous improvement – or kaizen. Without assessments of our leadership, we are sailing our ship without guidance. These assessments ensure that we are sticking to our vision for the organization; that we are being true to our philosophy of leadership; and that we are working on ourselves and with our team to be better.

Leaders Recognize their Fatal Flaw

Leaders have flaws. According to Zenger and Folkman (2009), about 30% of leaders have at least one fatal flaw. Regardless of the leadership skills or position a leader holds, we are human beings, and we aren't going to be perfect. No one expects their leader to be perfect, but they do expect their leader to be able to look critically at themselves, identify their flaws, and then create a plan to address them.

The one thing all leaders must avoid is succumbing to their fatal flaw. Zenger and Folkman (2009) explain fatal flaws are weaknesses that are so extreme that they can have a dramatic negative effect on a leader, seriously hampering their contribution to the organization and their career progress. Therefore, a leader's fatal flaw is that flaw which impacts the leader's ability to contribute or progress professionally. One's arrogance, for example, could be a fatal flaw if the leader is unwilling to listen to feedback. When it comes to the effects of these fatal flaws, blindness to the flaw has a steep cost (Zenger & Folkman, 2009). When a leader is unaware of or unwilling to see the flaw, the leader may pay the price; leadership in the organization will suffer because the leader is failing to be reflective and cannot envision the damage their flaw has on their leadership of the organization.

One of the greatest tools leaders have at their disposal can counter their fatal flaw: relationships. Colleagues who notice our weakness should be found and encouraged to speak. First, Zenger and Folkman (2009) suggest finding a truth teller who will provide honest feedback. Truth tellers are often referred to as "critical friends." Those are the friends that tell us when there's food stuck in our teeth, when we make a mistake, or when we need to hear difficult feedback. And, it's important to be explicit with these truth tellers that we are seeking honest information. This is not the time to have someone sugarcoat their responses. For example, many of us have been asked by a friend a question that – if we were to answer honestly – would hurt their feelings. It's tempting to tell a white lie, to tell them partial truth, or to sugarcoat our answer. But, being honest with our colleagues, and finding somebody to be honest with us, is vital in leadership; if someone sugarcoats our fatal flaw, then we're in trouble. If the truth teller seems overly cautious at first, Zenger and Folkman (2009) advise, we should encourage them to open up by being proactively receptive. Also, when a truth teller's observations are received receptively by the person being critiqued, the person is most likely to feel safe continuing to provide similar feedback.

If we can't find a truth teller within our company or it's difficult to find a colleague willing to provide this type of feedback, then Zenger and Folkman recommend getting outside help. If our company doesn't offer coaching or assessment, it might be a good idea to hire a coach or therapist. A coach may be able to help us gain a better understanding of our weaknesses and find ways to remedy them (Zenger & Folkman, 2009). Figure 6.3 includes a list of assessment tools that can provide feedback and help leaders to discover their fatal flaw (see Figure 6.3 for a list of assessment/feedback tools).

Figure 6.3

Feedback Tools

- John Maxwell 360 Degree Leadership Assessment (2020): https://corporatesolutions.johnmaxwell.com/blog/ the-360-degree-leadership-assessment-1/
- Xator Corporation Leadership Foundry (2020): https://www. leadershipfoundry.com/5-powerful-leadership-feedback-tools/

Note: This figure includes assessment tools that can be used by an organization to provide feedback to the leader. These tools would be completed by team members in the organization since a leader is not able to discover his/her/their own fatal flaw.

Regardless of which leadership assessment tool you use, knowing your strengths, weakness, and any fatal flaws will help you address a plan to tackle these challenges and provide an opportunity to improve your leadership skills.

Leaders Use Self-Assessment and Feedback

Leaders consistently use self-assessment and feedback to improve their performance, skills, and leadership. Being able to look yourself in the mirror to determine (1) whether you gave it 100%, (2) whether you could have done something differently, or (3) whether you did everything you possibly could have to help others, is critical. The mirror doesn't lie. Feedback is an important aspect that helps leaders know what they're doing well and where there are opportunities for growth.

Self-assessment can help leaders and their teams. There are several questions I use to conduct self-assessment of my leadership. When I am self-assessing, I ask:

1. What am I doing well that is helpful and impactful for our organization?

2. What am I not doing well? How do I improve/change?

3. What is one thing I need to stop doing immediately?

4. Who is one person I can help right now?

Being able to provide myself with an honest, reflective self-assessment can be such a powerful tool. A self-assessment gives a snapshot of how I feel I am performing and will assist in my own evaluation process. A self-assessment requires every leader to be reflective and allows for a growth opportunity.

Regarding feedback on your leadership, there are several great tools available for you on-line. These tools allow leaders to receive important feedback, as well as conduct self-assessment. Using these tools enables leaders to continue to grow and develop their leadership skills (see Figure 6.4). The leader must be able to provide and receive feedback to ensure both the leader and their organization are improving at all times.

Figure 6.4

Self-Assessment Tools

- Galford, R. M., & Maruca, R. F. (2011). The leadership legacy assessment: Identifying your instinctive leadership style questions 1-10 of 30. Your Leadership Legacy. http://www.yourleadershiplegacy.com/assessment/assessment.php
- Mindtools. (n.d.) How good are your leadership skills? Emerald Works. https://www.mindtools.com/pages/article/newLDR_50.htm
- Optimal Thinking.com. (2020). Leadership assessment questionnaire. OptimalThinking.com. https://www.optimalthinking.com/business-optimization/leadership-assessment/
- Zenger, J., & Folkman, J. (2013, August 12). The eight-minute test that reveal your effectiveness as a leader. Harvard Business Review. https://hbr.org/2013/08/how-effective-a-leader-are-you

---

Note: Use this list to find self-assessment tools available online.

An important concept to consider when self-assessing is being able to accept constructive feedback from ourselves and others.

Leaders Learn from Other Leaders. There are also opportunities to receive assessment of our performance from other leaders. I have already mentioned mentors and truth tellers. The valuable role each of my own mentors has played in my personal development as a leader in my community was shared in a previous chapter (see Chapter 4). In order for the mentoring to help me, I had to be open to feedback. I needed to never be defensive about my actions when receiving feedback from my mentors; otherwise, they wouldn't have continued to provide it to me. I have also found great seminars, books, training sessions, and podcasts that are available in order to help with my self-assessment. When I read these books, attend the trainings, or learn about leadership on my own, I often look into my own practices to find ways to improve. I also suggest creating a leadership group both inside and outside your organization, join a professional association, join a service club, or volunteer. All of these opportunities create a space for self-assessment and improvement. Take advantage of learning from others so we can continue our own learning.

Leaders Keep Two Hands on the Wheel at All Times

To close the chapter, we return to the metaphor of driving. There are many different ways to hold the steering wheel, and it is often determined by the weather. In the summertime, many people drive with one hand on the steering wheel since the weather is nice and they are unlikely to encounter hazards on the road. Once the weather turns a little nasty in fall or winter, some drivers switch from driving with one hand on the wheel to two hands; others continue to drive with just one hand. When the snow is coming down and the roads are slick, some drivers hold the steering wheel too tightly – driving white-knuckled – and lose control of the car. When drivers are taught how to drive, instructors tell them to use two hands to hold the wheel because it's the safest way to drive, but some drivers don't follow this simple rule. Ultimately, two hands on the wheel will be essential at some point when driving a car – and when leading our organization.

As a leader, we must always have two hands on the steering wheel, no matter what. There is never a time as the leader when we only have one hand on the steering wheel because we never know when the road conditions are going to change or when we're going to encounter something we didn't expect. It's not the time to panic; it's not the time to drive white-knuckled, either. Having two hands on the wheel before we are faced with difficulty will help us regardless of the circumstance. When we have two hands on the wheel, we ensure that we anticipate difficult situations, and we are ready to respond immediately. Two hands on the wheel are essential for defensive driving, and they are essential in leadership.

Another advantage of having two hands on the wheel is keeping our car between the rumble strip and the centerline. A goal as leaders is to keep two hands on the steering wheel and keep our car (i.e. our ship - ourselves, our family, our team, and our organization) out of the ditch when bad weather, an unforeseen circumstance, or something unexpected jumps out in front of us. We want to be ready at all times and keeping two hands on the steering wheel is our best chance to stay safe and be prepared for whatever may come our way.

Conclusion

In this chapter, we explored the challenges of leadership. In the action plan for this chapter, please think about how you will address difficulties and crises. The steps that were outlined to lead in crisis and establish a new normal could provide you with ideas for improving your leadership, and the suggestions to assess your leadership will help provide you with honest feedback. In the action plan included in Figure 6.5, please complete your steps to lead through challenges (see Figure 6.5).

Figure 6.5

Action Plan: Leading through Challenges

What are your three takeaways from this section?
1.
2.
3.
What are two strategies you will use to address challenges?
1.
2.
What steps will you take now? (Action Step for Leading through Challenges)

Note: In this figure, you will reflect on leading through challenges by developing an action plan and integrating new learning and strategies.

Relate your action plan to what you've learned about leading during challenging situations and crisis. This information, along with that shared in Chapter 5, will provide a lens as you relate to the personal stories and experiences in the next chapter.

Chapter 7: Leadership Insights and Experiences

In Chapter 5 and 6, tips and guidelines relating to leaderships were shared. Developing a clear vision, providing service to the team, continuously learning, reacting to crisis and challenge, and practicing self-care are all essential actions leaders must take in their lives. Establishing pieces of my leadership philosophy have helped me to examine these essential components of my own leadership.

I have learned personally about each of these components of leadership during my 30+ years in education. Through my coaching, teaching, and administrative work, I have learned what works for me and what doesn't work. I have also been able to learn from others – those in my life who are mentors, friends, and acquaintances, as well as national and historical leaders. I have continuously worked to improve my leadership skills by honing these components. My leadership roles and experiences have influenced how I view myself as a leader. In the following chapter, several personal and historical leadership experiences will be discussed in more detail.

Section 1 – FlagShip

A flagship is the lead ship in a fleet of vessels. The leader of the flagship is responsible for the entire fleet. In a family, the fleet may include a spouse and/or significant other and any children. With an organization, our fleet includes employees and other stakeholders. With our schools, the captain of the fleet (i.e. superintendent, principal, administrator, department chair) wants every student, faculty member, staff member, and parent to pull their weight on the ship. With every organization or company, the ultimate goal often is to become the flagship. When this happens, the business, education, industry, or government becomes a model for other organizations to look to for guidance and leadership.

Developing Your Flagship. As a leader I've had the opportunity to be the captain of several flagship organizations. The reason we had such incredible organizations is because of the clear vision leadership developed for the organization, as well as the people who were focused on serving others and who were willing to work toward excellence within the organization.

One example of a flagship organization that I've been a part of is the Freeman (WA) School District. As the Superintendent of the Freeman (WA) School District, I'm extremely proud of the fact that the district has supported growth among its teachers and staff. In the last six years, three superintendents have come out of our school district and we've promoted several teachers into administrative positions. Freeman is ranked in the top 10% of public schools in Washington, and boasts average math and reading proficiency scores that are higher than the state average (Public School Review, 2020). The district has won numerous state, regional, and national awards for academics, activities, and athletics, which include being named the #1 Rated High School in the State of Washington. The team that I work with at Freeman SD is one of the reasons the school district has become a leader in the state. High test scores, athletics, and other recognition have brought this small school district in Eastern Washington to the forefront in the state.

Other small districts have looked to Freeman for guidance and leadership, and we have been happy to provide our services. In public education, it's not a competition between districts (with the exception of sports); we all want students to succeed. And, helping other school districts to be better, simply means more students will leave those schools successful and contributing members of society. Therefore, I try to ensure that Freeman (WA) School District not only leads from the front, but leads from the middle and back, as well. A responsibility of flagship organizations is to be leaders – to help other organizations to be better. At Freeman, we have taken up this yoke. We want to help other leaders build their fleets, to improve their "ships," and to become flagship organizations, as well.

When leaders are able to develop a clear vision with their teams, develop strong relationships with team members, and model expectations, the team develops pride in the organization – and in their leader. Often, when flagship organizations emerge, those outside the organization can point to the leadership of the organization as a key factor for success. Jim Rohn often said, "We cannot change the weather or the winds, but we can change the set of the sails" (Avery, 2016), and in flagship organizations, the direction the team is sailing is determined by the leader. When sails are filled with wind (i.e. momentum, success, support), then the ship makes headway toward the destination. The leader can determine the success of the organization by creating the right conditions for the team to grow. When we are able to work with unselfish staff members who pride themselves on helping others, who are great teammates, and who will do anything to accomplish the mission of the voyage, then the organization has an opportunity to be a flagship vessel.

Section 2: OwnerShip

Providing an opportunity for the crew – whether it is a family, team, staff or company – to have ownership requires a trusting relationship, strong leadership and a beneficial partnership. Ownership is more than being the owner. Ownership means the belief that team members work – and take pride – as if they are the owners of the place. When the staff and team members have pride and commitment to a greater purpose than themselves, then they have ownership in the success of the organization, and when success is achieved, they know they were integral in making it happen.

Leaders Know How to Be a Great Boss. Supervisors, bosses, managers. Whatever we call them, most of us have one. Are you ready for some bad news? We are probably going to work for some terrible bosses in our life. They are going to be terrible people and/or terrible leaders, and they will be terrible at being our boss. It's okay. Are you ready for some good news? We are also going to work for some great bosses in our life. We will really appreciate our boss when they display strong leadership. We might even love and want to emulate our great bosses.

We actually need to have both good and bad bosses in our life so that we can compare the characteristics and determine what makes a good boss versus what makes a bad one. What is the difference between a good and bad boss? Why are the good bosses so good and the bad bosses so bad? We need to know what a bad boss does, so when we have a good boss we will appreciate them even more. Additionally, we will become a better leader when we're able to know the difference between a good boss and a bad boss. Anyone who's in a leadership position wants to be an excellent supervisor. Being exposed to both good and bad bosses allows us to take the very best from our good and bad bosses so we can avoid doing things we learned from our bad bosses. We've all learned as much, if not more, from our bad bosses. With bad bosses we know what *not* to do. With good bosses we learn they aren't really bosses, they are leaders.

In Figure 7.1, Doug Kaplicky describes the differences between a boss and a leader in a short poem that I love.

Figure 7.1

Boss vs. Leader

Boss vs Leader
Boss says "I"
Leaders says "We"
Boss Demands
Leaders Coach
Boss Takes Credit
Leaders Give Credit
Boss Uses People
Leaders Develop People
Boss Issues Ultimatum
Leaders Model Enthusiasm

Note: In this figure, I share a poem that compares and contrasts leadership with being a boss. This poem came from Doug Kaplicky: PositiveFocus-7Group (D. Kaplicky, personal communication, 2019).

Sir Ernest "The Boss" Shackleton. Let me share the story of Sir Ernest "The Boss" Shackleton who was an explorer, a leader, a hero—and ultimately an awesome man to work for. Every ship endures issues, concerns, and problems (Lansing, 1959). But with an effective captain, the crew will navigate the storms which come their way.

It was during the "Heroic Age of Exploration," when Sir Ernest Shackleton's 1914-1916 British Imperial Trans-Antarctic Expedition took place (Lansing, 1959). Antarctic expeditions often became ordeals of suffering, but Shackleton distinguished himself as a hero and earned the respect of his men, not to mention the respect of millions today, by being a leader who put his men's well-being, both mental and physical, above all else.

In January 1915, the *Endurance, Shackleton's ship,* became trapped in ice, ultimately forcing Shackleton and his men to vacate the ship and set up camp on the floating ice (Lansing, 1959). While Shackleton was called "The Boss" by his men, he did not differentiate himself from them. When the crew moved off of the debilitated ship to a camp on ice, Shackleton ensured that neither he nor his officers received preferential treatment. In an attempt to help his crew and get over the trauma of abandoning their ship, Shackleton served his men by developing a plan for their mental, physical, and spiritual well-being, including their physical activity, nutrition, and safety. Shackleton exhibited extraordinary leadership and helped his twenty-eight men survive nearly two years of unimaginable hardship at the end of the earth.

After the ship sank, Shackleton and his men crowded into three small boats and made their way to Elephant Island, off the southern tip of Cape Horn to escape Antarctica in April 1916 (Lansing, 1959). Seven hard days on the water culminated in the team reaching their destination, but there was still little hope of rescue on the uninhabited island, which, because of its location, sat far outside normal shipping lanes. Seeing that his men were on the precipice of disaster, Shackleton led a team of five others out on the water again. They boarded a 22-foot lifeboat and navigated their way toward South Georgia. Sixteen days after setting out, the crew reached the island, where Shackleton trekked to a whaling station to organize a rescue effort. On August 25, 1916, Shackleton returned to Elephant Island to rescue the remaining crew members. Astonishingly, not a single member of his 28-men team died during the nearly two years they were stranded (Lansing, 1959).

Shackleton distinguished himself from simply being the captain of the ship; he became the leader of a shipwrecked crew. He worked to ensure survival of his crew by sacrificing and taking on tasks to help in any way he could. Because Sir Ernest "The Boss" Shackleton took on the characteristics of a leader when his ship was wrecked near Antarctica, he saved many lives and earned the respect of his crew. He considered his crew's best interests and worked to coach his men into the mindset that was required to survive such severe conditions for such a long period of time.

Each one of us deals with hardship in our lives. As a leader, we will not only face hardships ourselves, but we will need to help our family, staff, teams, and organizations through these hardships. As we lead through hardship, we will question ourselves, our decisions, and our circumstance. I have experienced many hardship, such as losing friends, my parents, and students. Although these losses have been difficult, one of the greatest challenges I have faced in my life has been dealing with a school shooting and its aftermath - which will be discussed in more detail in my future work.

Section 4 - SportsmanShip

Most of us have heard the saying, "Be a good sport, win or lose." I believe this is such an important guideline for leaders. My dad told me as a kid, after we lost an important baseball game, "You win some, you lose some." My comment back was, "Yes, dad, I just didn't want to lose that one." However, whether we win or lose, as leaders it is important to be excellent role models on how to win and lose. This upcoming section will discuss several important aspects of sportsmanship.

Leaders Understand and Value Sportsmanship

Teams and group participation have been found to teach leadership skills, sportsmanship, and receptivity to coaching. Good sportsmanship builds teamwork and character, and teaches respect, honor, discipline, kindness, inclusion, resilience, and perseverance. No matter what group event we were involved in, the expectation was we were going to be a good team-mate. We were expected to play fairly, and we were also expected to exhibit other characteristics of sportsmanship, such as respect, honor, dis-cipline, kindness, inclusion, resilience, and perseverance. Lessons learned from teams and group participation can contribute to effective leadership because we learn to listen to others, provide suggestions and try our best, and work together toward a common goal.

As a leader, we most likely participated in some group events in our life, and these probably contributed to the development of our leadership skills. It could have been on a team or in a band. Maybe it was playing games, such as "Kick the Can" or some other game with family or friends. It may have even been playing organized sports, like baseball, soccer, or football.

As I grew up, I have already mentioned by involvement in baseball (see Chapter 4). I remember my experience from my days on the Kalispell Lakers American Legion Baseball Team. As a sixteen year-old, my friend David and I drove 20 miles one-way every day for baseball practice. This was after he had finished track practice, and after I had finished tennis practice. But, the long drive was worth it. Our team had great players and our coaches – George, Dave, and K.C. – were fantastic people and coaches. We traveled and played games all over the Northwest; I even played in eight professional baseball stadiums before I even when to college. This experience, and the players and coaches I played with and against, are memories I have cherished ever since. We didn't win every game we played, but we won with class and we lost with class. To this day, this experience taught me the lesson of sportsmanship that I carry with me.

The concept of sportsmanship applies to organizations, as well. In the prior section ("Flagship"), I discussed flagship organizations. And, although I strive to be the leader of such an organization, I also appreciate those organizations that are struggling or striving for the same. I support the leaders in other organizations, and my pride doesn't impact my will-ingness to help them grow. Being taught how to be a good sport has carried over to my leadership. I know that when I can surround myself with other great leaders, I will become better. It's not a competition anymore; more-over, when I help another organization become stronger, I take pride in helping them accomplish their goals even when I am struggling with my own.

Leaders Maintain a "Coachable" Spirit. When considering what sportsmanship looks like, being coachable is a characteristic that comes to mind. On teams, talent may seem like an important trait, but talent alone doesn't make someone a great athlete or teammate. Many talented people are unsuccessful on teams because they are not coachable. Consider the following questions:

- What are the attributes of a good coach?

- What are the attributes of being coachable?

- Are you coachable?

- Have you ever known someone who didn't want to be coached?

People are considered "uncoachable" because they thought their way was the right way, they knew everything, or they had all of the answers. Often, uncoachable people might try to succeed on their talent alone; they think they can win by themselves and don't consider the rest of the team in their actions. On the other hand, maintaining a coachable spirit means someone is willing and open to receiving coaching and mentoring, regardless of the situation. Since we are either getting worse or getting better at all times, our openness and willingness to maintain a coachable spirit sets us apart from others who think they have all of the answers. As a leader, we may encounter leaders who are uncoachable and also people on the team who are uncoachable. Regardless of the circumstance, dealing with a colleague or team member who is uncoachable is difficult.

Characteristics of a coachable spirit factor into facets of my everyday life. For example, on my team, we try to discover potential team members' coachability before selecting them to join our team. Every time we conduct an interview for an open position in the organization, we ask a question about the candidate's coachable spirit. With every answer I hear, we are able to have a very important conversation about coaching – both being a coach and providing coaching. Each of us needs a coach and when we have a coachable spirt, then we are willing to take input, we're open to suggestions, and we're able and willing to allow someone else to share things which can help us become better.

We all need a coach. Even the best athletes, leaders, and actors in the world have a coach. If you don't think you need a coach - you're at the end of your game. We don't know it all. We can always learn more, grow more and expand more. See Figure 7.2 for questions to consider about your coachable spirit (see Figure 7.2).

Figure 7.2

Coachable Spirit

1. Who are your coaches?
2. How do you respond to constructive feedback?
3. How do you maintain a coachable spirit?
4. Are there members of your team that are difficult to coach?
5. How can you help them to develop a coachable spirit?

Note: Use this figure to ask yourself questions about coachable spirit on your team and within yourself.

Having a coachable spirit, and having access to a coach or coaches, will help us maximize all of our opportunities. Every successful leader maintains a coachable spirit throughout their lifetime because they know for their teams and organizations to improve, the leader must improve first. Being open to feedback also helps leaders to avoid succumbing to our fatal flaw(s), a concept mentioned earlier in Chapter 6. Being coachable makes a leader better, and it means practicing kaizen.

As a leader, we want our family members, teams, and organizations to show good sportsmanship at all times. There are times when we win and there are times when we will lose. We can learn from both. We must understand the importance of treating all people with dignity and respect. We also understand our team will be watching us and our sportsmanship as well. When leaders act with good sportsmanship and are coachable, then they are a model for the rest of the organization. We are the models for our organization.

Growing Your Leadership

During Chapter 5, guidelines were presented for developing a clear vision, developing leaders on our team, self-care, and continuous learning. The steps to lead in crisis and establish a new normal, presented in Chapter 6, could provide each one of us with ideas to improve our leadership when faced with challenges. In this chapter, I shared personal leadership insights and experiences which can provide an opportunity to reflect on your own personal experiences. In the action plan for this chapter, please think about how each of these factors influence your leadership. Use Figure 7.3 to plan for growing your own leadership (see Figure 7.3).

Figure 7.3

Action Plan: Leadership II

What are the strengths in your leadership? 1. 2.
Which characteristics from Chapter 5 and 6 do your leadership experiences demonstrate? 1. 2.
Describe a part of your leadership that could be stronger. What are some steps you can take to improve this component of your leadership?
Which of the elements that impact leadership do you plan to work on going forward?

Note: Use this figure to reflect on personal experiences that could help you to grow your leadership.

By being able to critically analyze our own leadership, we create the space for growth and development. Only those leaders that are willing to see themselves in the mirror, including the strengths and weaknesses, will be able to improve their teams and create "flagship" organizations.

Chapter 8: Partner*Ships*

"Alone we can do so little; together we can do so much."

Helen Keller (Lash, 1980)

We have all probably heard the traditional proverb, "Two heads are better than one." A partnership is all about cooperation. Every family, team, and organization works better with a successful partnership in place. Leaders and their teams may be part of several partnerships. Partnerships are built from a combination of relationships and leadership, brought together through connections that are mutually beneficial.

An example of partnership is a marriage. A marriage involves give and take. Each person enters the partnership with their own values, principles, ideas, and beliefs. Deciding things like where you're going to live, where you will work, how many kids you and your spouse will have, how you plan to raise your children, and how you handle finances are important for every marriage. Unfortunately, coming to agreement on some of these items is difficult. According to marriage and family counselor, Dr. John Gottman (1999), 69% of marriage conflicts are never solved. This statistic implies spouses often have the same fight over and over again. In order for a partnership to work, the partners must decide how to resolve conflict so that each partner is satisfied with the outcome. Knowing the pitfalls and challenges that can negatively affect a marriage is important. Marriage isn't always easy and there are times in marriage when partners aren't on the same page, in the same book, or even in the same library.

As in a marriage, professional partnerships rely on working through challenges, treating on another with respect, and working toward a common goal. To build a successful partnership, according to Rhett Power (2018), organizations should follow four tips:

1. Set clear expectations.

2. Consider your partner a part of your team.

3. Give the partnership room to grow.

4. Make honesty and transparency your watchwords.

Power (2018) claims that following these tips will set up the partnership for success. These tips will be described in more detail throughout this chapter.

Partnerships Develop Operating Principles

Clear expectations are the cornerstone to a strong partnership, and successful organizations and partnerships are the result of effective and dynamic leadership. To assure a quality operation, leaders must agree on basic ways of operating together. Operating principles define the beliefs, values, and methods of working together. The manner in which the leaders and their team conduct their business becomes a model throughout the organization and serves as an example for staff and our "customers" of how problems are solved.

The Freeman School District School Board and Superintendent have developed our own operating principles. In Figure 8.1, the Freeman School District Board – Superintendent Operating Principles are included (see Figure 8.1). The main concepts of honesty, loyalty, and disagreement; communications, cooperation, and support; decision-making; and communication are used to provide clear categories for the principles the district has adopted.

Figure 8.1.

Freeman School District Board - Superintendent Operating Principles

---

Honesty, Loyalty and Disagreement

A sustained commitment to a group, person, or organization survives and is nurtured in an open environment that recognizes the need and right of the parties to construct, express, examine, and synthesize divergent thought. Understanding opposing viewpoints helps us to better represent our interests.

We accept the challenge of pursuing a common intent through a review of opinion and fact, to an end that is understood and defensible by all. Once a final decision is reached, each member will support the decision.

By way of fulfilling our commitment to the challenge, we agree:

- To be honest at all times.
- To support each other constructively and courteously.
- To maintain confidentiality.
- To allow ourselves and others the freedom to admit mistakes.
- To focus our discussions on issues, not personalities.
- To pursue thorough understanding.

Communications, Cooperation, and Support

Open communication requires trust, respect, and a fundamental belief in goodwill among team members. We will work to minimize misunderstandings and reduce conflict by:

- Supporting each other constructively and courteously.
- Maintaining confidentiality.
- Focusing our discussions on issues, not personalities.
- Constructively dealing with disagreement.
- Upholding the integrity of every individual.
- Pursuing thorough understanding.
- Involving parties who will be affected by the decision and solution.
- Expressing our opinions and positions on issues honestly and openly while being sensitive to others' opinions.
- Avoiding promotion of individual agendas.

Decision Making

The identification and evaluation of alternatives, awareness of short- and long-term consequences, and appreciation for the needs of the group, as well as individuals, and sensitivity toward collective action are essential to the decision-making process.

In order to formulate and execute sound decisions, we agree to:

- Resolve problems at the lowest level possible.
- Provide for input from all concerned when possible.
- Use a decision-making style appropriate to the situation.
- Engage in respectful deliberation as decisions are made.
- Reevaluate the effectiveness of the decision when appropriate.
- Communicate decisions that are made with clarity.

Using this process, we recognize a decision may sometimes be superseded by a higher level of authority. When this occurs, the rationale will be communicated to those involved before releasing the information.

Communication

Listening expresses our concern for others by showing an interest in not only the information but also the other person. Active listening benefits each party and is a key to effective communication. We should take sufficient time to summarize and paraphrase what we have heard.

A healthy climate for communication requires trust, respect and a fundamental belief in the goodwill among team members. Messages need to be open, honest, and tactful. We work to minimize misunderstandings and reduce conflict. We strive for mutual understanding and support.

As a leader/leadership team, we make the following commitments:

1. Keep the tone and demeanor of discussions professional by avoiding defensiveness and personalized anger.
2. Demonstrate that we have recognized the other's point of view.
3. Share information with all people affected in a timely manner.

Figure 8.1. The Freeman SD board-superintendent operating principles (2013a).

The agreements and commitments made by the district and its partners make it clear that common goals have been established for the relationship between the school district and its stakeholders.

Teamwork

When creating a partnership, the partners need to ensure that both parties can participate in decision making, and that each party is able to benefit from the partnership. Unlike some other relationships (i.e. bosses/employees, mentors/mentees, teachers/students), a partnership should always be mutually beneficial for both parties. And, in order for the partnership to work, potential conflicts must be addressed right from the start.

The Freeman SD Board – Superintendent Operating Principles are an example of how partners can work together. These guidelines provide a framework for the school board and superintendent as they work with community partners to create a space for students to learn and grow. The operating principles take into account the various ways the school board interacts with the superintendent in regards to decision making, communication, cooperation, support, and disagreements. This creates an even playing field for all partners since expectations for behavior and interactions are clearly laid out.

Growth

One of the benefits of a partnership is that it pools resources so that both organizations can grow as a result. Extending the breadth of each teams' resources is a vital way to increase the potential of each organization. Team members, monetary resources, and other resources can be shared to increase each organization's ability to meet the goals of the partnership.

For example, a university that partners with a marketing firm can increase its enrollment in online courses substantially. This benefits both entities because (1) the university gains students in its program and tuition and (2) the marketing firm gets a cut of the profits from the new students. Both partners benefit from the partnership, and by extension, experience growth in their organization. By sharing resources, and expertise, the partnership is able to also benefit students who now have access to an online program that may not have existed without the partnership.

Honest and Transparent

Partnerships need to be based on trust and honesty – just like all relationships (see Chapter 3). This also means letting a potential partner know your organization's shortcomings prior to the partnership. This enables the potential partner to enter the relationship with both eyes open. By knowing the strengths and shortcomings of the partner ahead of time, each organization can determine if the partnership is a best fit for both.

Going back to the university and marketing firm example. If the university had told the marketing firm they had all of the faculty on board to create online courses by a certain timeframe, but in reality, hadn't talked to the faculty or did not have qualified faculty on staff, the lack of transparency would damage the partnership. The marketing firm was operating under the assumption all courses could be offered by a certain time, and the fact the university was not upfront might damage the marketing campaign. If students think they can start in Fall 2020, but cannot start due to classes not being prepared, this could also damage the university's reputation. Being upfront about the lack of faculty buy-in or qualified faculty might have allowed the marketing firm to adjust the admission deadline and in turn, their advertisements.

Obviously, honesty and transparency are essential for a successful partnership. Without these two characteristics, the partnership is not based on trust, and a lack of trust will doom the partnership to failure.

Taking Inventory of Your Partnerships

In order to see exactly where you stand with your partnerships, a list of current partnerships is helpful. Ranking each one on a scale of 1-10 (10 being the strongest), based on how you perceive your relationship with them can help take inventory of each partner. To get you started, use Figure

8.2 to list five of your current partnerships and rank them 1-10 (with 10 being the strongest partnerships and 1 being the weakest) (see Figure 8.2). Use the four characteristics of partnerships suggested by Power (2018) to determine your rankings.

Figure 8.2.

Current Partnership Rankings

Partnership	Ranking
1.	
2.	
3.	
4.	
5.	
Why did you select these five?	
How did you decide the ranking for each one?	

Note: Use this figure to take inventory of some current partnership relationships. Use a rating scale of 1-10 (10 = strong partnership and 1 = a partnership that needs work).

As you listed each of these five partnerships, think about your partnership with each one as they connect to relationships and leadership. Do you have a partnership with them because you had a relationship first? Do you feel the leadership with these partners is a strength for their organization? The reason we don't usually partner with someone or something is because we don't have a relationship with them. We certainly aren't going to partner with a company that doesn't have great leadership. We will partner with someone we don't have a great relationship with beforehand, but we won't partner with someone who has questionable leadership.

Prospective Partnerships

Once you've determined your current partnership list, build your prospective partnership list. This new list includes any partnership (i.e. person or organization) that would be mutually beneficial for both organizations. Your selection isn't a decision connected to who could benefit, this is a decision connected to the partnership working for both parties. Use Figure 8.3 to brainstorm some new partnerships that you'd like to develop (see Figure 8.3).

Figure 8.3

Prospective Partnerships

Prospective Partner	Benefit for Your Organization	Benefit for the Partner
1.		
2.		
3.		
4.		
5.		
Why did you select these five?		

Note: Use this figure to brainstorm a list of possible partnerships that you are interested in developing for your organization.

How would this new partnership be mutually beneficial? In what ways would it be mutually beneficial?

As you continue to build your list of additional prospective partnerships here are a few questions to ask a prospective partner:

- What do you need?
- How can we support and help each other?
- How can we enhance our partnership?

Developing a process to recruit, enhance and grow new partnerships has additional benefits. You and your prospective partner can help build on each other's strengths, help fill the areas where one party needs additional support, and find a way to help elevate both organizations.

Conclusion

In this chapter, we were able to explore the importance of partnerships. We also took inventory of current partners and brainstormed a list of potential partners. In the action plan for this chapter, please think about how you will reflect on what you learned and develop some ideas for improving your partnerships. Using Figure 8.4, please complete your steps to take action regarding your partnerships (see Figure 8.4).

Figure 8.4

Action Plan: Partnerships

What are your three takeaways from this section?
1.
2.
What are two strategies you will use to improve your partnerships?
1.
2.
What steps will you take now? (Action Step for Partnerships)

Note: Use this figure to develop an action plan for improving your partnerships.

These takeaways and strategies can help you with ideas improving your partnerships. Successful partnerships are able to withstand the test of time. Knowing how to build, cultivate, and strengthen partnerships, you can work together for years to come.

Chapter 9: Partnership Insights and Experiences

As we reflect on relationships with people who have helped us in our lives, we may or may not have viewed the relationship as a partnership. Whether it be with a family member, a staff member, someone we bought a car from, or someone we worked with on a project – our partnerships – those relationships that have been mutually beneficial to each party - have helped to create something greater than we could have by ourselves. Understanding the benefits of any partnership creates a synergy where the combined effort is greater than the individual effort. My partnerships have not only positively impacted my partners and those I serve; they have positively influenced my leadership abilities. In the following chapter, I will share stories of my partnerships and famous partnerships in order to provide insight into the complexities of creating successful partnerships. As I discuss partnerships in more detail, consider how each demonstrates the four characteristics of partnerships mentioned by Power (2018): (1) clear expectations, (2) teamwork, (3) growth, and (4) trust. Each of these characteristics are essential for partnerships to succeed.

Section 1: ColleagueShip

In a professional environment, we are able to build relationships over time, and we begin to build a partnership with colleagues, which I call "colleagueship." Bonds built between individuals on teams, groups, or organizations, provide an opportunity for people to become part of a partnership that, often times, stays in place for the remainder of our lives. Because we often have strong interests in common with our colleagues, the partnerships that are formed in a professional environment are often stronger than many casual relationships we might have with friends outside of work. Sharing common goals can contribute to a strong partnership relationship at work.

An example of colleagueship in my professional experience is the partnership I have formed with several other superintendents in my area. For the past nine years, I've been part of the Spokane Valley Superintendent Group which includes the superintendents from the Central Valley School District, East Valley School District, Freeman School District, and West Valley School District. We meet at least once a month, sometimes more, to collaborate, brainstorm, and share ideas on how we can help support the students, families, staff, and communities that bind us together. Our four school districts serve approximately 23,000 students, and all four school districts are connected geographically and by school district boundary lines.

As we have exchanged ideas throughout the years, we have come to realize we are better together. Even though we differ in size, our mission is the same – to serve our students, families, staff, and communities. Our four school districts have helped each other with levy campaigns, learning plans, career and technical education services, special education services, and financial operations. We support each other when one of the school districts has completed a new building or project, and one of the greatest examples of our partnership is Spokane Valley Tech, a program offering opportunities to students in all four school districts.

One thing I'm really proud of us is how our colleagueship has helped each of us become better leaders, while also becoming closer personally. We work together to mutually benefit each school district, individually, and as a group, and it has also helped us all improve our skills, abilities, and resources.

The Microsoft Marriage. An excellent example of a business partnership, and a model for many leaders, is the Microsoft Marriage.

Microsoft co-founders Bill Gates and Paul Allen first met as teenagers in the late 1960s at Lakeside School in Seattle, when Gates was in eighth grade and Allen was in tenth grade. It was a computer terminal that first brought them together. Computer terminals were rare at the time, but Gates and Allen were able to access them by helping the owners of a computer store. They worked out a deal with a local company to use the computers for free if they would help identify problems. This is what led to the first official partnership between the two – and between the computer store owners. Gates and Allen were able to work with and learn from the computers, and the store owner was able to receive technical services. Both parties benefitted, and both had a clearly outlined vision of how their relationship would work.

Gates and Allen continued working together after high school. In 1974, the summer after Gates' freshman year at Harvard, they were both computer programmers at the software company, Honeywell. In 1975, when Gates was 19, he dropped out of his sophomore year of college to launch Microsoft, now a trillion dollar company, with Allen. They developed a partnership built on common interests. Although their relationship started before they even graduated from high school, they built one of the largest companies in the world by having a clear vision, using teamwork, being honest and forthcoming, and giving one another room to grow. Their collaborative spirit and ability to build their partnership has forever changed the world of technology. Because their relationship was strong from the start, the partnership was able to flourish. This example provides other leaders with a model to build their own partnerships.

Section 2: ChampionShip

Championships are often the goal of organizations, but in partnerships, we also have to work toward mutually beneficial relationships. Championship teams can provide these types of relationships to their organizations, their team members, their fans, and their community. Championship leaders focus not only on the final game itself, but on creating "champions" of the players on their team. This concept also relates to creating a "team" with your partner (as mentioned in Chapter 8). When partners create clear roles, both teams can flourish and both teams can benefit.

One example of a championship partnership is John Wooden, the most successful basketball coach in NCAA history, and the partnerships he created with his players. Wooden taught young men at UCLA to play basketball and more importantly, how to live successful lives. Wooden is best known for winning 620 games, 10 NCAA titles, including seven in a row from 1967 to 1973; being named NCAA College Basketball's Coach of the Year in 1964, 1967, 1969, 1970, 1971, 1972 and 1973; and in 1973, being honored in the Basketball Hall of Fame as a coach and becoming the first person to be honored in the Hall of Fame as both a player and a coach. But, Coach Wooden's most important contributions came from the principles by which he coached and lived his life. Here is Coach Wooden's "Seven-Point Creed":

1. Be true to yourself.
2. Make each day your masterpiece.
3. Help others.
4. Drink deeply from good books.
5. Make friendship a fine art.
6. Build shelter against a rainy day.
7. Pray for guidance and give thanks for your blessings every day. (Wooden, 2005)

Although Wooden's list includes many principles that focus on the individual, there are some, like "help others" and "make friendship a fine art" that speak to creating relationships and partnerships. Wooden was a partner with his team, and he valued fellowship among his team. He wanted to win, but he knew that in order to lead, he needed to help his athletes grow their own leadership skills. The relationship he had with his athletes was mutually beneficial.

There are many reasons I included Coach John Wooden in this section on partnerships. One of those reasons is my autographed picture of Coach Wooden and his "Pyramid of Success" (Wooden & Harrick, 1995) which is one of my most prized treasures. Wooden's "Pyramid of Success" is a guideline for leadership and partnership success. It includes the components: competitive greatness, poise, confidence, condition, skill, team spirit, self-control, alertness, initiative, intentness, industriousness, friendship, loyalty, cooperation, and enthusiasm. I have been able to use the pyramid in my own life. The second reason is Coach Wooden was an excellent partner: he was a teacher, a coach, a mentor, a leader. You are a teacher, coach, mentor, and leader, as well. To become an excellent partner and to develop a championship team, one of your main responsibilities is to ensure you partner with your team to become the best. This opens the door for you to help others become the best they are capable of becoming. Coach Wooden was a champion because he built the right partnerships. He worked with athletes he knew he could shape into leaders upon graduating; he worked with the community to ensure he had the resources he needed; and he worked to create a culture of support and fellowship.

Teaming with Your Partners

As a former Head Baseball Coach, I understand the importance of the partnership developed by a team through their teamwork. When a coach is counting on a team of twenty-five players, one begins to understand the importance of each player, the coaching staff, the statisticians, the trainer, and the managers. The coach realizes that without all of these "partners" the team would not be successful. As coaches gain more experience, they also begin to understand the importance of the umpires, the parents, and the fans. Everyone on a team has a role, and the partnership needs to be mutually beneficial for the team to be successful.

Every one of us is connected to a team, and in connection, a partnership. Teamwork is the collaborative effort of a group to achieve a common goal or to complete a task in the most effective and efficient way. I believe every successful team is centered on effective teamwork and these five guidelines:

1. Have a clear vision of where they are going

2. Have open and honest communication

3. Have high levels of trust

4. Have defined roles

5. Have an interest in the "bigger picture"

Following these guidelines will help to contribute to a strong partnership. The people we create partnerships with become part of our team, and when combined, we are stronger than we were apart.

Big 3. One of the college coaching classes I took from Dr. Warren Friedrichs discussed Coach Twamy's "Big 3" (W. Friedrichs, personal communication, 1987). For success, Twamy said you have to have 3 things: The Horses, the Knowledge of the Game, and the "Esprit de Corps." The "horses" are our players, our team members. Every company or organization needs "the horses" - the horsepower - and there are three types of horses: the stallions and mares, the brood, and the nags. Every good coach, every good leader, makes their decisions based on their stallions and mares - the coach's leaders. Leaders don't make decisions on the nags; otherwise, the stallions and mares get disenfranchised and upset with the leader. There are two ways to improve our horses - "our team" - we either improve the horses we have or get better horses. Horses can be developed within our own team, but through a strong partnership, we may gain access to talent and leaders that we may not have access to otherwise. By pooling resources, partnerships can create opportunities for both teams.

Every leader has to ensure their "horses" learn the knowledge of the game. In other words, our team needs to know their job and they need to know how to do their jobs well. Relating to partnerships, this means having a clear vision and clearly defined roles. When the team knows their job, they can work toward the goals established through the partnership.

We need a staff who know, and want to learn, as much as they can about what they are doing, about their position on the team, and the importance of the team. Their improvement helps the entire organization improve. Knowledge is a powerful tool to help individuals and every team be their very best.

"Esprit de Corps" is the most important of the three. "Esprit de Corps" is French for the spirit of the corps, or the feeling of pride, fellowship, and common loyalty shared by members of a particular group. "Esprit de Corps" really means teamwork. When an individual understands putting the interests of the team ahead of their own interests, then the individual is committed to and understands the importance of the team. Teamwork brings the horses and the knowledge of the game together. In a partnership, working toward a common goal helps to establish a clear meaning for the partnership. But, in order to create a strong team, the players need to feel trust in one another and know that communication is open.

A team with all three has a very good chance at a highly successful partnership. If you pay close attention to most championship teams, oftentimes the champion isn't the one who is the best team. The teams who won the most championships, whether it is in education, business or athletics, is usually the team who plays best as a team. There's a big difference and as the leader, our ability to understand how Twamy's "Big 3" affects our team, will allow our organization or company to have the most success.

Learning to Coach – And to be a Better Partner. When I first started coaching over thirty years ago, I wasn't very good at it. I thought I was good, but in reality, I learned more as a coach every single year. I didn't realize at first that I needed partners on the team. When I look back on those first few years, I can see everything much more clearly. Even now, I know that I can still improve as a coach, and I continue to work on ensuring being on the team is mutually beneficial for those involved. It's the same with leading. There are some days, after over thirty years in education, where I'm not very good at leading my team. I want to be great every day, but some days I forget to listen, to trust my team, and to share control. I'm still working on my coaching and leadership skills. Every day, I work to create stronger partnerships with my team and its stakeholders.

Think back on your experiences. Think about the teams you have been a part of. Were those teams mutually beneficial for those involved? How were all of the voices listened to and heard? Think about the very best things from each team and each coaching staff. What made the teams successful or unsuccessful? Think about teams you are currently a part of. Are you applying the principles of partnerships to the teams you are on today? As you continue to develop your team, maybe you still need to improve your coaching skills – maybe you still need to work on your ability to partner with others – maybe you need to work on being a better partner. I recommend staying focused on your team and on your improvement. By practicing the key skills for successful teams: a clear vision, open and honest communication, high levels of trust, defined roles, and an interest in the "bigger picture," your partnerships – and your teams – will improve.

Section 3: Customer ServiceShip

Serviceship often refers to a hybrid between service learning and traditional internships in school; however, in this section, I refer to serviceship as the relationship between the leader or organization and those served. Serviceship provides opportunities to people on the team in order to promote growth and leadership development. The relationship between service and *The 3 Ships* is clear, and serviceship is the perfect word to describe this relationship.

In retail, customer service means providing timely, attentive service to customers while making sure their needs are met in a manner which reflects positively on the company or business. Maya Angelou (2012) once said, "I've learned that people will forget what you said, people will forget what you did, but people will never forget how you made them feel." Even though Angelou wasn't referring to customer service directly, this quote illustrates the importance of creating a space where people feel valued.

Good customer service means taking care of our customers like we want to be taken care of. There are plenty of examples of great customer service to learn from.

Dealership

The partnership between the Coeur d'Alene (ID) High School administration team and Parker Toyota and its owners began through family connections, since their children attended the school. Our team developed both a relationship and a partnership with Jim Parker and Mike White as a result of shared interests. Parker Toyota shared their leadership model with us and their customer service plan. We copied these plans and standards from Parker Toyota. Our leadership team abilities and customer service at Coeur d'Alene High School improved dramatically, thanks to Jim and Mike.

Throughout the years Parker Toyota has been able to help support different organizations and give back to the community. They understand their partnership with the community and two of their events include the Perfect Attendance Spells Success (PASS) Program and a Car Giveaway. PASS is an incentive based program for public elementary students in the Coeur d'Alene, Lakeland, and Post Falls school districts to attend class every day in their last year of elementary school. As a reward, Parker Toyota will donate a bike and helmet to each graduating elementary student who has perfect attendance during the school year. PASS encourages students to set goals as a way of life. When the program started in 2005, approximately 50 students received a bike and helmet. Over the past couple years Parker Toyota added Parker Subaru to the program. Together, this raised more awareness and increased the amount of bikes they were able to deliver to the kids. Also, every year Parker Toyota donates a car for students from Coeur d'Alene High School and Lake City High School so they can conduct a car giveaway. The two competing high schools sell raffle tickets to the community in an effort to raise funds for their athletic programs. This becomes a highly competitive, yet friendly, competition between the two schools. One lucky winner takes home a brand new Toyota, Last year the two schools raised over $100,000 and since the inaugural event, Parker Toyota has raised over $1,000,000. All of the money stays with the high schools. These are two of many examples where Parker Toyota's partnership with the local community and organizations has made a difference.

As a family, we have personally bought our last four vehicles over the last 15 years from Parker Toyota for three reasons: the first reason is our relationships with Jim, Mike and their team. The second reason is their leadership, which directly impacts customer service. Our salesman, Jeff Smith, is a professional. He's a professional person and salesman. Jeff is the epitome of customer service. The third reason is because of our partnership with Parker Toyota. Even after moving out of the area we had a choice: have our vehicles serviced locally or stay with Parker Toyota. We chose to stay with Parker Toyota and will continue to stay with them. Parker Toyota is a model for relationships, leadership and partnerships.

Section 4: CommunityShip

Henry Mintzberg coined the term "communityship" as "a process of social influence in which everyone in a community exercises leadership" (Mintzberg, 2013). This means, to me, that everybody in the partnership shares in the leadership, and there is an openness among the members of the team regarding input and ideas. Using the guidelines for leadership, partnership teams can consist of many different communities we are a part of, and when we are able to apply the traits of effective partnerships to each of the communities we work with, we will be able to develop stronger relationships with each.

Non-profit Partners

There are several non-profit organizations that can serve as partners in the community. Schools serve as the hub, or center, of many communities. Schools provide a foundation of learning for children ages 3 -21, but besides learning about academics, children learn about relationships and social-emotional learning, are involved in activities and athletics, and are connected to teachers and other influential adults. Schools thrive due to their partnerships with the community. Churches are another great community partner. Used for religious activities, particularly for Christian worship services, churches are located throughout the world and were created to provide people with a physical location to meet. Although churches vary in size, style, and location, they are role models for partnerships in a community. Churches often serve their communities as places where members can turn to get assistance, attend support groups, as well as receive spiritual guidance. Nonprofit groups are another great example of community partnerships. These organizations are dedicated to providing support or furthering a cause. These organizations often exist to provide services to their communities, and partnerships with community nonprofits can be a great source of fulfillment for both parties – the relationship is mutually beneficial because of the service provided.

Government Partners

Government agencies are necessary partners in many businesses and organizations. In some cases, this partnership can be frustrating and may not exhibit the characteristics of effective partnerships. However, in some cases a government partnership can be extremely helpful for us and our organization. It may not always feel mutually beneficial, but most government agencies were established to help the community they serve. Working with local, state, and national governments means the partnership might not always be equal for both parties, but with a goal of teamwork and benefitting all partners, a government partnership might be a great relationship to cultivate.

There are four main types of local governments - counties, municipalities (cities and towns), school districts, and special districts - that might provide partnerships. Each of these local governments could provide an opportunity for partnerships with our organization. Often, these smaller, local governments are more approachable and there is less bureaucracy to navigate in order to establish a partnership. For example, counties are the largest units of local government, numbering about 8,000 nationwide. Municipalities include cities, villages, and boroughs and number about 19,000 in the United States. Most of the more than 15,000 school districts in the U.S. operate independently of city government, and 33,000 special districts nationwide are organized to provide one or more services such as water and sanitation, mosquito control, transportation, parks and recreation, or flood control. Each of these local governments have the power to create partnerships with organizations in their communities, and since school districts, special districts, municipalities, and counties consist of much smaller groups of people and a smaller area, they might be even more invested in creating local partnerships that will benefit those they serve.

Beyond local government, each state in the U.S. has their own government, and the federal government of the U.S. also exists to serve its constituents. Each of these forms of government are larger, and require more investment on both parties in order to create partnerships. Within these larger forms of government, organizations often need to establish relationships with different people of divisions of the government. For example, the teacher preparation programs in Washington have a relationship with several state organizations in order to run their university programs effectively. First, the university has a partnership with the Washington Association of Colleges for Teacher Education (WACTE) is an organization that partners with programs throughout the state, meeting tri-annually in order to establish norms among and across the teacher preparation programs. This organization works closely with the Professional Educator Standards Board (PESB), which is a government agency that establishes the standards for teacher certification and testing across the state. In addition, the universities, WACTE, and PESB work with the legislature to ensure that laws are passed to support teacher education programs.

This partnership is essential for the programs to be effective, for the programs to understand their goals and standards, and for everybody to be on the same page with future teachers in our state. Additionally, the teacher education program and principal programs have an advisory board that consists of local teachers and leaders in the community surrounding the university. This board provides feedback to the university regarding community needs, and also provides feedback on the university's performance in teacher and administrator preparation. Each of these partnerships are essential for the proper functioning of the university programs, and each of the groups benefits from the partnership. WACTE benefits by having all teacher preparation programs in the state in the same room, and this provides a venue to share ideas and program changes. PESB is able to work as a liaison with the programs, WACTE, and the legislature to be responsive to the needs of students and the government. And, members of the advisory board help the university to be better, while the university helps the community by providing new programs and responding to local needs. In this example, one can see how a partnership can involve several organizations working together for the benefit of all.

Business Partnerships

Partnerships may also involve business collaborations. When partnerships are created between companies or between businesses and government organizations, those partnerships can be used to finance, build, and operate projects, such as public transportation networks, parks, and convention centers.

Some partnerships that can be created with local businesses include the Chamber of Commerce or local banks. The Chamber of Commerce is a business network whose goal is to further the interests of businesses in the local community. It might benefit a local business to partner with the school or for two local businesses to create a partnership together. A Chamber of Commerce usually has a board of directors or executive council, who then hires a leadership team. The Chamber of Commerce has the larger community goals in mind, and through their leadership team may be able to bring together businesses that might not have worked together otherwise. Banks and credit unions are another local business that could provide a great partnership. These for-profit financial (i.e. corporate banks) institutions and nonprofit (i.e. credit unions) financial institutions provide services such as checking accounts, savings accounts, business accounts and offering loans. There are many banks and credit unions that offer grants, scholarships, and other community services. Partnering with a bank or credit union on a project is often beneficial for both parties – even if the benefit for the bank or credit union is simply good publicity.

Growing Your Partnerships

In this chapter, we were able to explore our partnerships through personal and professional insights and experiences. In the action plan for this chapter, please think about how you will address the importance of your leadership as it connects to partnerships. Use Figure 9.1 to reflect on your own partnership insights and experiences (see Figure 9.1).

Figure 9.1

Action Plan: Partnership Insights and Experiences

What are the strengths in your partnerships? 1. 2.
Which characteristics from Chapter 7 and 8 do your partnerships demonstrate? 1. 2.
Describe a part of your partnerships that could be stronger. What are some steps you can take to improve this component of your partnerships?
Which of the elements of your partnerships do you plan to work on going forward?

Note: Use this figure to develop a plan for your partnerships.

Refer to Powers' tips for developing strong partnerships as you consider the strengths and characteristics of your own partnerships and your potential partnerships. Whether you'd like to establish partnerships with colleagues, your team, community partners, businesses, or government agencies, following simple guidelines will help your partnerships to be successful going forward. You will be able to create a "championship" team by improving relationships with partners.

Chapter 10: Captain of Your Ships

"The capacity of the organization can't be exceeded
by the capacity of its leader."

Zenger Folkman (Zenger & Folkman, 2009)

As a leader, there are opportunities for each one of us to step up our leadership impact. We can either lead positively, with love, care, support, and appreciation for our crew, or we can lead with an iron fist with no care or concern for those we lead and serve with. Throughout this text, I have share stories, guidelines, and research related to relationships, leadership, and partnership: the three ships. This book can guide readers to become stronger in all three of their ships.

One of the themes that emerged from this book was reflective practice. Through my life – and while writing this book – reflecting on my relationships, leadership, and partnerships has helped me to become better at all three. Only by constantly reflecting and improving have I been able to be part of so many "flagship" teams during my career. I learned early in life that relationships were the key to everything, and in order to be a leader or to a partner, I had to start with strong relationships. To this day, I feel blessed that I've been able to work with and be around so many great people who have taught me what it means to be a friend, a teammate, a mentor, a husband, a father, a son, and so many of the other roles I have taken on throughout the years. Only by reflecting on each of my relationships have I been able to improve myself, and in turn, lead and improve others. My beliefs about reflection influence each of my ships, and I hope that throughout this book, these beliefs have become yours. I truly believe when one starts reflecting regularly on their experiences - on what went right and what went wrong in every situation, on who we need to work harder with to establish a stronger relationship, on how to improve ourselves – everything else will fall into place. You will be happier because your three ships will stay on course and you will be able to sail them smoothly toward your destination. I choose to lead with love, care, support, and appreciation for those I'm serving. I hope you will join me as we are constantly reminded that the captain of any ship is only as good as their crew.

To plan your route and bring your three ships toward your desired destination, I developed these ten thoughts about building your ships. I use these guidelines to help myself as I work toward improving my three ships.

1. Build and develop your current relationships

2. Build and develop new relationships

3. Build and develop your leadership skills

4. Build and develop your team member's leadership skills

5. Build and develop your current partnerships

6. Build and develop new partnerships

7. Build and develop your mentoring skills

8. Build and develop your team member's mentoring skills

9. Identify your plan to build a "Better and Bigger" Ship

10. Identify your replacement - A New "Captain" of The Ship

These simple steps can guide you as you move toward creating stronger relationships, leadership, and partnerships in your organization. This chapter attempts to bring together the main concepts from this book and leave the readers with a takeaway that can propel them forward in their journey.

Lessons Learned

Over the course of history, leaders have learned important lessons about keeping their ship afloat. As the Captain, you must pay attention. Keep your focus on what you and your team are doing at all times. Use your leadership skills, and learn from others, and don't let anything sink your ship. As you have read this book, you have learned or been reminded of many things a leader does, as well as some of the things a leader must not do. As a successful leader, knowing the difference between what to do and what not to do elevates your leadership. With elevated leadership skills and abilities, your team will elevate as well. A rising tide will lift all boats. Be a rising tide for everyone around you.

Considered to be unsinkable, the Titanic was the largest and most luxurious cruise liner of its day. It was also declared by some to be the greatest ship ever built. However, on the night of April 14, 1912, the Titanic struck an iceberg and sank, killing more than 1,500 passengers. Here are a few lessons we can learn from the Titanic that will help every leader as you captain your ship:

1. Any Ship Can Sink - there is no such thing as an unsinkable ship. As you think about your relationships, leadership and partnerships, remember any one of them can be destroyed. The captain provides for, protects, and leads their ships at all times.

2. Trust Your Crew - your crew is your family, team and organization. Every crew member has an important role on the ship. Each voyage needs a crew who works together. Trust and communication will either strengthen you and your team or it will break you apart.

3. Prepare for Your Journey - every voyage requires planning and preparation. It's important for the Captain and the crew to have the correct equipment for the journey and use the equipment available.

4. Have a Destination - you and your crew need to know their destination and have an itinerary for your trip. The captain and crew work together so there are no wrong turns and you reach your destination safely.

5. Stay on Course - Every captain has a crew and a compass. There is no need to guess where you think you might be going. It's important for the Captain to pay attention to the information you have from your team to make adjustments and stay on course.

Although all leaders will make mistakes during their careers, there are many mistakes which could be avoided. Rely on your team as much, if not more, than you rely on yourself. Use the lessons learned from the Titanic, as well as other learning opportunities, so you will keep your ship afloat.

Bringing Your Ship into the Harbor

The 3 "Ships" spotlights the importance of developing your relationships, leadership and partnerships during your lifelong journey. As you have read this book and completed the assignments at the end of each chapter, you should start to see a change. This change in yourself is a result of the reflections you've written and questions you've considered. You are different now and because of this change you will now think about your relationships, your leadership, and your partnerships differently. These changes will not only have positive implications for you, they will have a positive impact for all of your teams. As the captain, you understand your team won't be better than your leadership. You also understand bringing your ship into the harbor is a collaborative effort.

As the Captain of your ships, you have made incredible headway, learning as you travel from port to port. Even though you will have to navigate rough waters - there is no reason to be afraid. You need rough waters in your life just like you need to know about bad captains and how to tackle crises and challenges. Rough waters will help you to develop and improve your skills as a captain. You now realize the captain is the helper.

As captain, your number one priority is to help others; you are here to help your family, your team, and your organization. The more you help others, then the more impact you will have on them.

With *The 3 Ships* you are ready for the next voyage in your life. You are now ready to fulfill your true desire - to be helpful, be an encourager, and be someone who makes a difference in the lives of others. How can you help as many people as possible? How can you make a difference in the lives of everyone on all of your teams? By using your three ships.

Action Plan and Next Steps

As the fable goes, Noah said he could only take two animals on the Ark. Here is a question for you, "What two leadership concepts or ideas would you contribute to the leadership Ark of life?" You can only contribute two. What would they be?

At the end of several chapters, you were asked to write down your three takeaways, two strategies to improve, and one action step. Then, you were asked to analyze your experiences in relationship to the characteristics of relationships, leadership, and partnerships that were described in each section. These activities allowed you to:

1. Read the information

2. Think about and analyze the information

3. Reflect on this information

4. Prioritize the information

5. Take action

Leaders take these five steps every day, sometimes twenty times a day, sometimes a hundred times a day. Remember, the learning occurs upon reflecting on what you have learned, done, or experienced and then making yourself better. As my good friend and mentor, Dr. Rich McBride, says, "Never forget – you've had the power to do this all along" (R. McBride, personal communication, April 9, 2020). When you take action to make yourself better, then you are committing to making your family, your team, and your organization better.

Conclusion

As we bring this chapter, and book, to the end of our voyage together, you are now ready to take your leadership to the next level. By taking the information, stories, and research, along with reflecting on your skills, abilities, and opportunities to be a better captain, you are ready to put your action plan into motion. Taking your next steps as the captain of your ship will help you and crew – whoever that may be – take your relationships, leadership, and partnerships to the next level.

References

Alvy, H. (2017). *Fighting for Change in Your School: How to Avoid Fads and Focus on Substance.* Alexandria, VA: ACSD.

Anderson, E. (2012, December 17). *Abraham Lincoln: 10 quotes to help you lead today.* Forbes. https://www.forbes.com/sites/erikaandersen/2012/12/17/abraham-lincoln-10-quotes-to-help-you-lead-today/#6e1c736a110a

Angelou, M. (2012). *The collected autobiographies of Maya Angelou.* New York, NY: Random House.

Avery, C. (2016). *The responsibility process: Unlocking your natural ability to live and lead with power.* Pflugerville, TX: Partnerworks, Incorporated.

Bidwell, L. (2020). *Why mentors matter: A summary of 30 years of research.* SAP SuccessFactors. https://www.successfactors.com/content/ssf-site/en/resources/knowledge-hub/why-mentors-matter.html

Bundrant, M. (2019). *The importance of communication skills demonstrated through 10 studies.* INLP Center. https://inlpcenter.org/importance-of-communication-skills/

Coleman, K. (2020). (Executive Producer – Dave Ramsey). (1992-present). *The Dave Ramsey Show* [Audio podcast]. Lampo Licensing, LLC. https://www.daveramsey.com/show/archives

Definition of Kaizen. (n.d.). Kaizen Institute. https://www.kaizen.com/what-is-kaizen.html

Freeman School District. (2013a). *The Freeman SD board-superintendent operating principles.* Freeman, WA: Freeman School District.

Freeman School District. (2013b). *The Freeman SD expectations for employment.* Freeman, WA: Freeman School District.

Goman, C. K. (2011, August 1). *The six levels of trust.* Forbes Media LLC. https://www.forbes.com/sites/carolkinseygoman/2011/08/01/the-six-levels-of-trust/#8afa41c6fb79

Gordon, J. (2018). *The Power of a positive team: Proven principles and practices that make great teams work.* Hoboken, New Jersey: Wiley.

Gottman, J., & Silver, N. (1999). *The seven principles for making marriage work: A practical guide from the country's foremost relationship expert.* NY: Three Rivers Press.

Harrick, J., & Wooden, J. (1995). *The pyramid of success: Championship philosophies and techniques on winning* [Audiobook]. Lexington, KY: Wyncom Incorporated.

Hersey, P., & Blanchard, K. H. (1982). *Management of organizational behavior: Utilizing human resources.* Upper Saddle River, New Jersey: Prentice-Hall.

Influence (n.d.). Vocabulary.com. https://www.vocabulary.com/dictionary/influence

Lansing, A. (1959). *Endurance: Shackleton's incredible voyage.* NY: Basic Books.

Lash, J. P. (1980). *Helen and teacher: The story of Helen Keller and Anne Sullivan Macy.* NY: Delacorte Press.

Leman, K., & Pentak, B. (2004) *The way of the shepherd: Seven secrets to managing productive people.* Grand Rapids, Michigan: Zondervan.

Martinuzzi, B. (2019, October). *The 7 Most Common Leadership Styles.* https://www.americanexpress.com/en-us/business/trends-and-insights/articles/the-7-most-common-leadership-styles-and-how-to-find-your-own/

Maxwell, J. (2011). *The 5 levels of leadership: Proven steps to maximize your potential.* NY: Center Street.

Moore, K. (2013, June 7). *Henry Mintzberg interviewed by Karl Moore - excerpt* [Video]. Youtube. https://www.youtube.com/watch?v=Gg461YRSyfM&feature=emb_logo

Power, R. (2018). *4 Ways to Build a Successful partnership.* Mansueto Ventures. https://www.inc.com/rhett-power/4-ways-to-build-a-successful-partnership.html

Reis, H. T., & Sprecher, S. (Eds.) (2009). In *Encyclopedia of human relationships* (Vol. 2) (pp. 951-954). Thousand Oaks, CA: Sage.

Taibbi, B. (2018, October 20). *5 keys to successful relationships: Like strong houses, good relationships need a solid foundation.* Psychology Today. https://www.psychologytoday.com/us/blog/fixing-families/201810/5-keys-successful-relationships

Tello, M. (2017, November 16). *Self-care: 4 ways to nourish body and soul.* Harvard Health Publishing. https://www.health.harvard.edu/blog/self-care-4-ways-nourish-body-soul-2017111612736

Weir, K. (2017). Forgiveness can improve mental and physical health: Research shows how to get there. *Monitor on Psychology 48*(1), 30.

Wooden, J., & Jamison, S. (2005). *Wooden on leadership: How to create a winning organization.* NY: McGraw-Hill.

Zak, P. J. (2017, January/February). The neuroscience of trust. *Harvard Business Review*, 84-90.

Zenger, J., & Folkman, J. (2009, June). Ten fatal flaws that derail leaders. *Harvard Business Review.*